THE WOMEN OF
PLAS YN RHIW

The Women of Plas yn Rhiw

Mary Allan

ISBN: 0-86381-881-1

Cover Design: Sian Parri

Published by
Gwasg Carreg Gwalch,
12 Iard yr Orsaf, Llanrwst, Wales, LL26 0EH.
Tel: 01492 642031   Fax: 01492 641502
email: books@carreg-gwalch.co.uk
website: www.carreg-gwalch.co.uk

Printed and published in Wales.

Contents

Contents

Chapter I

Y Plas – Early History

The village of Rhiw centres defiantly on a bleak saddle between the hog's back of Mynydd Rhiw and Mynydd y Graig, which derives its name from a perpendicular rock descending from a conical peak. The village is often enveloped in mist and is almost always subject to fierce winds, mainly from the south-west. A minor road from Aberdaron, on the tip of Llŷn, is joined by an even more minor one that girdles Mynydd Rhiw from the north. From this road, a tree-lined lane leads down the mountain to the western end of Porth Neigwl. On this lane stands Plas yn Rhiw.

Some half-way down the hillside, the site offers a complete contrast to the bleak village above. Sheltered from all winds except the south-easterlies, it nurtures centuries-old woodlands of native trees, which in their turn surround and protect the Plas. This seclusion further enhances the equable climate of Llŷn and enables plants to flower all the year round in the gardens, so that stepping through the gate on a winter's day is like stepping into spring. Although they are usually beneath a shroud of hill-fog, sea-mist or low cloud, they are usually clear enough to permit a view. From the upper windows of the house, the visitor can see Pen Cilan on the far side of Porth Neigwl (*Hell's Mouth*) and look out over Bae Ceredigion. Occasionally he can glimpse St David's Head and the islands off the west coast of Pembrokeshire.

A little way up the hill, to the north, are the remains of the earliest known inhabitants of this part of Wales. A track leads to an isolated farm-house, from whose yard two low walls converge on a foot-path, barely wide enough for two men to walk abreast, leading straight up the mountain. At the top are two stone barrows. Nothing else remains to tell who was buried here, but the approach and the fact that there are two cromlechs suggest people of some importance. Further north again was a stone-axe factory supplying a large part of the British Isles. This all implies that from the earliest times of human occupation the mountain was recognised as a good habitation like Mynydd y Graig and other mountain-tops to the north and east.

Overlooking Ynys Môn, the whole western coast of Wales and parts of Ireland, it was an ideal spot for Meirion Goch of the royal line of Powys, to settle when he was sent by his grandfather, the king, to watch for marauding Norsemen. It was to him that the Lewis's, the first known owners of the Plas, traced their origins.

Sixteen thirty-four is the earliest date inscribed on the house, and it was probably about this time that the Plas, in its present form, was erected by John Lewis. This would have consisted of the south-western end forming the parlour, the spiral stairs and the western end of the hall on the ground floor, with bedrooms above and a loft for the servants on the top floor. A document copied from the

8

Caernarfonshire Court of Quarter Sessions, is displayed in the house and refers to the son of John Lewis – 'Richard Lewis in Rhiwe' as the owner in 1643.

Nevertheless, the very thick walls of the gable end suggest an earlier building, later incorporated into the Jacobean. Early in the eighteenth century, a *croglofft* cottage was built at right angles to the house, possibly as a dower house. By the nineteenth century, this was used as a bakehouse and laundry. At present it has been restored as a holiday cottage. Later in the eighteenth century, the house itself was extended by the addition of a large kitchen, with a storeroom and another room above. The stairs were moved and a partition erected to give a small parlour as sitting room at the southern end. The removal of the bottom flight of the spiral staircase left an alcove which the Keatings thought at first to be a priest-hole, since Llŷn was one of the last bastions of the Old Religion. There is no evidence for this.

At the beginning of the nineteenth century, the heiress, Jane Ann Lewis, married William Williams. Her daughter, again the heiress, married Captain Lewis Bennet, who soon afterwards set about enlarging the house. The date 1820, together with the initials LMB, was inscribed on a lead weight from one of the sash windows, which the Keatings discovered during their renovations of 1940. About the same time, the roof was raised to provide a second storey attic. The alteration is clearly visible on the outside walls today. A verandah was added to the front of the house; the windows were enlarged and the walls stuccoed to give it the appearance of a Regency manor house.

When Captain Bennet died in 1850, it was his grandson

who inherited. He never married and at his death the house passed to his half-brother, thus extinguishing the direct line of succession. Debts accrued, part of the land was sold off and the house itself was sold to a Mr Roberts, whose son let both house and land. One of the tenants of the house was Lady Strickland, who used it for summer holidays. She is credited with planting the box-hedges in the garden, to shelter it from the south-east wind.

The last tenant left in 1922, after which the house and garden fell into disrepair until the Keatings bought them in 1939.

This, then, was the state of 'abandoned neglect' as Honora called it into which the property had fallen through the lack of interest of the owner. Even the sale had to be conducted through intermediaries and they never came into contact with him.

Unsurprisingly the garden was a wilderness of overgrown trees, shrubs and brambles. The sisters had to hack a way through to the house and only gained entry by climbing up to the first-floor windows. A stream entered by the back door and flowed out through the front. Dry-rot was everywhere. But their friend, the architect Clough Williams-Ellis, pronounced the roof sound, so they went ahead. To them it felt like coming home.

Immediately, they set about making the ruin habitable. They replaced the rotten floorboards; they renewed the staircase; they added the oak pillars in the hall; they put in new plumbing and installed a huge copper boiler for central heating in the kitchen. They brought furniture and furnishings from Nottingham and supplemented them by attending country-house auctions. They also inherited pieces from other branches of the Keating family. Soon it resembled the interior which visitors see today.

As to the exterior, they wished to emphasise the earlier history, rather than the Regency period in which it had been encapsulated. To the dismay of some architectural experts, they decided to remove the stucco and expose the stone walls beneath. Yet the verandah remains as do the Georgian windows. The result is an idiosyncratic but charming mixture of styles. The explosion of a land mine on the rocks of the bay below, which cracked the plaster, gave added impetus to this restoration. Not all of the house is open to the public. Most of the top floor and about half of the first floor forms a flat for the resident Administrator. The rest of the house gives a good impression of what it was like when the Keatings lived there.

Opening off the verandah, the front door gives immediate entrance into a dining hall floored with green slate, as advised by Sir Clough Williams-Ellis. Family portraits overlook eighteenth and nineteenth century furniture dominated by a massive eighteenth century gateleg table. In the far corner is set a side-door opening onto the courtyard. This door is Gothic in design and reputed to have come from nearby Madryn Castle. It, and the oak pillars to give a feeling of antiquity, were also suggested by Sir Clough. The step down in the middle of the room is the demarcation between the original building and the eighteenth century additions.

To the left of the hall is the Parlour, the Keatings' sitting-room. Here they entertained their special friends, and where Honora painted her water-colours. The grate has a bread-oven. By the side of it is a door closing off the place where the bottom flight of the spiral staircase has

11

been removed. This was the space which the sisters first thought was a priest-hole.

Behind the hall is the kitchen, another eighteenth-century addition, which has its own door leading out to the courtyard. As in Welsh farmhouses, this was where the main work of the house was done. In the Keatings' day, it was dominated by the huge copper boiler, of which they were extremely proud since it supplied the central heating on which their comfort depended. Outside the kitchen door is a flight of stone steps, used by the sisters while the indoor staircase was being restored, and possibly afterwards, too.

The eighteenth century staircase was so badly rotted when the Keatings took over the house, that it had to be completely replaced. Now it is decorated by several works of art on its walls and landings, but the most interesting are the water-colours by Honora, mostly of local scenes. Mainly in blues, yellows and beiges, they reflect the fashion of the twenties and thirties.

At the head of the first flight of stairs is a small room furnished as a library. Occupying most of one wall, is a bookcase crammed with volumes written by friends such as Teresa Hooley and R.S. Thomas. In this room Honora drafted business letters for Eileen and conducted their various campaigns.

Next to this, at the front of the house is the large sitting-room, where official guests were entertained to afternoon tea. Directly above the parlour, it shares the spiral staircase. A door in the corner opens onto the steps climbing to the top floor. To its left is a small bedroom – the Yellow Bedroom – sharing the same awe-inspiring views of sea and mountains – the subjects of many of

Honora's water-colours, speaking of her love of Llŷn and its clear light.

On the top landing is a grizzly reminder of the sisters' declining years – the medicine cupboard containing remedies of the day. Opening off the landing is Honora's bedroom, with the end of the spiral staircase. The Japanese prints on the walls are a reminder of her 1939 voyage. Next-door is a smaller bedroom and on the other side a small staff-room. Incised into its window, as with a diamond ring, are the initials A.W. Could these have been done with an engagement ring belonging to Jane Ann Lewis, trying out her new name when she would be married to William Williams? Or could they have been those of Miss Wright, companion to Miss Roberts, daughter of the last owner of the Plas before it became a ruin?

In the garden, the nettles, brambles, thistles and smaller weeds have given way to ordered abundance. Flowers bloom all the year round in the shelter of the mountain, the house and the box hedges which survived the neglect sufficiently to be restored. Delphine Drouhin roses twine round the pillars of the verandah to welcome the visitor with fragrance and colour; fuchsias enjoy a lengthy season on the flagstones below; a rosa mundi droops over the path to the house. The glory of the whole is the magnolia mollicomata planted by Honora in 1946, which covered in white, star-like flowers in April, and is twisted, conical red fruit in August. It was here that Honora toiled, on her return from work in England to exhaust herself and repair her nerves, tangled by bombs and overwork.

Among the usual outbuildings is one whose original

purpose is shrouded in mystery. The Vicar of Bodedern, the Rev. Edgar J. Jones, writing in *Yr Herald Cymraeg* in 1961, describes how Miss Lorna went to this building, a little to the north of the house, to fetch leaf-mould for the garden. She was surprised at the number of passers-by who called it Yr Hen Gapel *(The Old Chapel)*. They didn't know the reason for the name of what was to them an old cow-shed, but architectural features suggest a Pre-Reformation date and a superior use. It is just possible that it was indeed a chapel of the Old Faith, when the pre-1634 house was still standing. It remains derelict, its roof long fallen in, but a link to the past which is otherwise only found in the thick walls of the western end of the house.

Chapter II

Up to 1918

The early history of Nottingham records a pleasant custom. The city was surrounded by countryside and the townspeople would walk out to view the flowers that grew there, especially the crocuses, at the end of winter. No wonder, then, that the girls born there to John William Keating and his wife Constance Annie, were to show throughout their lives a love of the countryside, and especially of wild flowers. These girls, Eileen, born in 1886, Lorna, in 1890 and Mary Honora, in 1892, were to become cherishers and protectors of a different countryside long before this became fashionable.

Their father, an architect, was the son of a railway official, and a member of a large family whose daughters attended the Nottingham High School for Girls in force in the late Victorian and Edwardian periods, according to the school magazine. The Keatings believed their ancestors had been Irish, but an enquiry at the Dublin College of Heraldry in later years, seems to have failed to establish their right to a coat of arms. At least, they did not subsequently lay claim to one. Nevertheless, they seem to have lived in some comfort and an early photograph shows them posed outside a pleasant villa.

Their mother was the daughter of Edward Wood, who is described on their aunt's marriage certificate as a 'lace manufacturer'. Possibly the Woods considered themselves socially superior to the Keatings on account of this prominent position in the city's leading industry. A letter from John William to Constance arranging a meeting in the garden at six a.m. suggests the need for secrecy, at least at the beginning of their courtship. After the marriage, there seems to have been no hostility, with gifts, greetings and visits being exchanged frequently.

A hint of tragedy comes in the photograph of a little boy, apparently lying in his shroud. There is no note on the back as to who this child is, but its inclusion in the archive would suggest a brother who died in infancy.

A greater tragedy occurred in the death of John William Keating in his early forties, when Honora, the youngest, was only a baby. By then, he had become so eminent locally, that he was voted a Freeman of the city. His Dimension Books of 1889-2 show him doing valuations for building societies and the Foresters, but his greatest contribution to the life of the city was his planning of the fashionable houses in the Park.

Despite his death, the family remained comfortably off. Already, in his lifetime, the father had begun acquiring property, including some in Castle Chambers. His widow administered it with advice from her solicitors and later with help from her daughters. This task occupied them for the rest of their lives, but made possible their life in Llŷn, which was the one by which they became better known.

Their daily lives were much like those of any well-off family in Nottingham. They had servants, learnt the piano, kept pets and led a full social life. Eileen noted in 1901, 'About 15 parties last year . . . more the year before'. On Sundays they attended High Pavement, a leading Congregational Chapel adorned by a stained glass window by the pre-Raphaelite painter, Edward Burne-Jones.

No record remains of their early education, but Eileen and Honora at least were sent to secondary schools. Eileen attended Hollygirt School, where she wrote poems, one on Snowdrops and another on Queen Mab, and a plot for 'Cinderella'. In the Sixth Form she studied Scripture, Music, Mental Arithmetic and Physiology and achieved the school's Certificate of Merit in 1904. She did well in most subjects, but not outstandingly in French, although her mother noted in 1897 'that she goes to Miss Stevenson with Madge for French'.

Honora's secondary school was the Girls' Public Day School Trust Nottingham High School for Girls. Here at the age of 14, she wrote a sentimental essay about animals and flowers, and in the Sixth Form a story about gypsies. The final achievement of her academic career was a 'letter' in English and History with distinction. Both show promise but clearly her main talent was for art. Each year from the Lower III onwards she earned commendations and prizes from the Royal Drawing Society.

In the Upper Fifth, a sheet of her pencil drawings was included in the RDS's Exhibition at Fishmongers' Hall, highly commended in the First Class. In the same year as the 'Letter' she was awarded a Silver Star and two Bronze Stars. The examiner was Professor Henry Tonks, Head of the Slade School of Art in London.

From the time they left school, the careers of the eldest

17

and youngest of the sisters diverged, yet they kept in close touch and often helped each other.

Before she was twenty, Eileen must have gone to France to live with a family as an au-pair or nanny, for there is a letter to her from France in a childish hand (dated 1908) declaring that the writer 'loves her very much' and describing how he's been 'hunting' with his father. The following year there was a letter signed 'Louise' containing a photograph designated 'Colette, Claire and Marguerite, Mme. Kerleau and her children'. Eileen became a lifelong friend of Colette, who was a member of a large family, with a holiday house on the Ile de Bréhat, off the western coast of Brittany. It seems likely that Eileen went to them first as an au-pair or nanny, in the hope of improving her French. A notebook contains French phrases, which she must have been trying to learn. One, at least, suggests the nanny, 'Will you take her to change her?'

In subsequent years, she went over in the summer taking Lorna with her. The two English 'misses' became members of the family. A postcard from Bréhat in August 1912, enquired when they were coming over that summer, and they were in Brittany at the outbreak of World War I. On 6th August they received official permission to reside at Bréhat, but were not to move. But by the 28th of the month they received permission to return home.

During these same years, Eileen started helping her father's sister, Emma Keating, who ran one of the many small private schools in the city. Born in 1867, she was artistically gifted, as drawings by her at the ages of twelve and thirteen attest. She never married and lived to the end of her life at Caythorpe, not far from Nottingham. All three sisters seem to have been devoted to her.

By the midsummer term of 1913, Eileen seems to have branched out on her own, and to be running a kind of 'evening school' in which she taught French, recording payments for lessons in an old exercise book. Lorna is said to have helped her, though the nature of this 'help' is not specified.

Honora took a very different course. By 1913, she was enrolled as a student at the Slade, living at College Hall, Byng Place, a hall of residence of London University. In a letter written for the School Magazine, she describes life at the Slade and her life as a young girl in the Capital, walking its streets, going to concerts, observing everything. Her drawings preserved from this time show meticulous attention to detail and also definite ability. She might well have become a famous painter had not the War intervened. She left the Slade to join the Women's Land Army between 1918 and 1920 (acting as one of its Welfare Officers). Entries in her register of the girls in her care showed that she looked after them conscientiously, noting the recreations and visits. Thus, she was preparing herself for her final post in World War II.

In the early part of their lives the Keating women seem to have taken holidays in different parts of the country. In 1891, a correspondent of Eileen's describes herself as 'your Skegness friend'. About 1902, Mrs Keating took Eileen with her on a holiday to Newhey, for convalescence after an illness, as she wrote 'the air is doing me good'. They were apparently staying in a boarding-house, but they seem to have indulged in plenty of social life, going to tea, receiving invitations and playing croquet. They also went for long walks and found a bird's nest, marsh marigolds and bluebells. Eileen sent some of these home to Honora, who was urged to go to bed early and keep up her practising. Apparently neither wrote to Lorna. In 1913, Honora went for a holiday to Llŷn and fell in love with it. Later she brought her mother and sisters there and they took various cottages in the neighbourhood of Aberdaron and Rhiw. This little-known part of Wales was to become their home.

If Aunt Emma Keating influenced Eileen's early choice of career, and Honora probably inherited her artistic gift, there was another aunt, the mother's sister, who may have been the model for Honora's complete change of direction after the War. This was Alice Wood, known to her nieces as 'Aunty Pop', who in 1887 married, very suitably, Percy James Cropper, a lace warehouse manager. Mr Cropper seems to have been a member of a prominent and forward-looking family, for someone with his surname, gave and later published a lecture on Women's Rights.

By 1912, Mrs Cropper had moved to live in Falmouth where she took cuttings from a Falmouth newspaper, containing home hints. She remained there until nearly the end of the War, by which time she had become Lady Superintendent of the Falmouth Division of the St John's Ambulance Brigade. Then, at the beginning of 1918, it seems likely that her husband died, and she obtained testimonials from the Cornish County Director of the VAD the Mayor of Falmouth and others, recommending her for a commission in the WRNS. Whether she was accepted is not known. A badge engraved with the Scottish Women's Hospital among her remains, suggests that instead she joined this determined band of women.

When she left Falmouth in 1928, she marked the

occasion by donating a Hammond Organ to St Biddulph's Church. She kept up a correspondence with several of her friends into old age, from her new home in Nottingham.

Chapter III

Inter-War Years – the older Keating women

There is little record of the activities of Mrs Keating and her two elder daughters during World War I. Possibly they felt there were more important aspects of life than keeping records of all their financial transactions and letters to and from friends. Possibly the records for those years are lost – buried under the tarmac of the Plas car-park.

At least, after the War, Eileen was able to resume her visits to Bréhat, and further afield. In August 1917, her friend Andrée had written to tell her that she was expecting a child, and expressed her unhappiness at being separated from her husband, Jean. In December 1918, she wrote to say that they were reunited and overjoyed that the war was over. By the 15th March of the next year she wrote to say she was happy to see Eileen again, although her little boy had nearly died and his sister, Alex, had broken her arm. By October 1921, full intimacy had been re-established and she wrote a long letter describing a family feud over the wrongdoings of 'Papa'.

Claire wrote from Quimper, complaining of seven years of sad life. Colette, she said, had been 'trop nerveux' but was now much better. Colette herself wrote to Eileen in June 1919, looking forward to seeing her at Bréhat, though she would have to wait, as Grandpère was very ill and expected to die soon. Then they would be able to go to Bréhat and she could rejoin them.

Jean Revol, who wrote of himself as Eileen's 'naughty boy' sent her a letter from Tunisia, where he was with the Army. He hoped to follow his father in business, and to spend a year in Manchester, where he would no doubt have made contact with the Keatings. Probably this didn't happen, because in May 1921, he wrote from New York, announcing his engagement, and thanking Eileen and Lorna for their kindness to his mother and sisters.

There were visits further afield as well. In 1925, Eileen's passport was stamped for France, and with it there was a map of south-east France, together with a bus timetable. Probably there were introductions to other members of the Bréhat family and connections which she was able to follow up. An Italian concert programme made it likely that one or more of the Keating's girls went to that country also.

At home, Mrs Keating had resumed the kind of life she led before the War. Her Rent Books for 1923 and 1924, attest her close attention to the property she owned. In 1923, she made further purchases of houses in Cranmer Street. In 1928 a crisis arose when she was faced with the repayment of mortgages of nearly £5,000, but was saved from having to sell by the maturing of an insurance. Her daughters helped her; in 1922, a letter from a correspondent giving his reasons for non-repayment of a loan was addressed to Eileen. Nevertheless Mrs Keating continued to oversee the administration and upkeep of her property, concerning herself even with details such as a Water Account of £2.18.0 in 1934 for her houses in Cranmer Street and Hounds Gate, and an extract from a lease for a shop covering certain repayments. In 1935, meters and electric light were installed in Castle Chambers and 14 Cranmer Street. The same year she paid £25 for new plumbing in Peveril Drive, as the old, according to the plumber, was 'past repair'. Insurance cover, too, for servants as well as buildings had to be provided.

Apart from her income from property, there was a considerable income from shares. Wisely she spread her investments, and was in constant correspondence with several stock-brokers. Among her shares were those of Ford of Dagenham, and later in 1936-7, those of Baird TV Ltd., and a local cinema. Looking after these must have taken a considerable amount of time, even with the help of Eileen and Lorna.

There were holidays, and Llŷn seems to have become more and more popular. The daughters are still remembered there as fashionably dressed young ladies. They rented self-catering cottages where they could entertain friends. A life-long friend, the poet, Teresa Hooley, who had a story published in the journal *Light* in 1919, described herself as 'of Aberdaron'.

Most interesting is a notebook of Eileen's listing addresses in France, Austria, England, Italy, Czechoslovakia, Spain, Switzerland and Poland. Interspersed with these are comments such a 'gave English to' followed by the names and ages of children.

An envelope containing cuttings describing children's games point to one of her methods in these 'lessons'. A letter from a friend in Switzerland suggests this was how she financed her travelling abroad. It tells her how the friend's daughter is acting as a governess in a Colonel's family, thus saving her parents the expense of her keep.

Some of the addresses are annotated. Under 'Ile de Bréhat' she describes a house as being let at 2000 francs 'pour la saison'. Doubtless her activities as the daughter of a propertied widow would have given her an interest in the price. At Geneva she notes that 'Honor and I stayed for Congress'. The only indication of the nature of the Congress is a list of societies helping mothers and children, especially Jews, and descriptions of cases of TB and their cures. She may well have been there as a companion to Honor, for the sisters often helped each other in ways which used their particular strengths. Possibly it was on this occasion they walked to Pilly, near Lausanne, between sessions or when the sessions were over. Here, too, she may have met Carlita Muttese, listed as 'Déléguée du Tribunal pours Enfants de Madrid'. On the other hand, her friendship with Carlita, with whom she corresponded for many years, may have been what led her to Geneva. It's startling to think that Eileen, brought up in a comfortable middle-class house in Nottingham, might have been helping Jewish mothers and children flee from the Nazis, but it would be in keeping with the strong sense of duty with which the Keating sisters confronted difficulty and distress. Nor would she have been the only woman similarly placed who took a hand in mitigating the effects of Hitler's growing strength in Germany.

In 1933, Carlita wrote Eileen a long letter in French, expressing among domestic details, her unease at the way politics were developing in Spain. After that, there were only postcards, ending in 1937 with one stamped 'Censurada'.

Annecy was important to Eileen as a place where she could go and teach in a school. The bus time-table for south-east France would have helped her find her way there and possibly she did stay there for a while, but there is no other confirmation of this; unless a cryptic note about a 'lady who helped me with the difficult young man' refers to this interlude. One would love to know how the young man was being 'difficult'.

Nevertheless, they had time to look outside their own concerns, and in 1931 they received acknowledgements of letters on the same day from Sir Herbert Samuel, the Home Secretary, and the Prime Minister, Stanley Baldwin. What the occasion was is not clear, though probably it concerned the disposal of the Clifton Estate, outside Nottingham. At least it gave the sisters practice in conducting a campaign – valuable when it fell to them to raise a petition about something they felt passionately about.

All this time Mrs Keating seems to have suffered various bouts of ill-health. Sometimes she resorted to cures other than those of her GP, Dr Rowe. In 1930, she requested someone who described himself as a 'Health Specialist' to waive her payment, as the treatment had done her no good. In 1932, she had to have a prescription from an optician, but complained to Eileen that her spectacles were not strong enough. A friend sympathised with her in a letter over her bunion and cystitis. No wonder she needed holidays in Llŷn!

It was during one of these, in 1934, that Mrs Keating broke her hip, and could not be conveyed back to Nottingham. From then on, she stayed in Llŷn, and one or other of the sisters had to be with her. When the mother of one of her pupils wrote to Eileen, asking if she would be able to bring her mother back after her illness, Eileen replied that Mother was 'able to walk a little' so it would seem that Mrs Keating was more disinclined than unable to return.

From then on the family began to take a greater interest in what was happening in Llŷn. The most important event in 1936, was the setting fire to buildings at Penyberth, near Pwllheli, by three Welsh nationalists, led by Saunders Lewis. The Keatings strongly supported this symbolic action against the building of an airfield on the site, since it was felt locally that it would militate against the Welsh way of life. Between March and May of the following year, they corresponded with the Air Ministry, protesting against the noise of the bombing-school associated with the airfield. Located at Porth Neigwl, it was just below Plas yn Rhiw, which was eventually to become their permanent home.

They considered other large houses on the Llŷn, one of these being Carreg Plas, which came on the market at this time. Another was Gelliwig, the empty former home of Miss Lloyd Edwards who became Mrs Gough of Nanhoron. But they had already, in 1934, considered buying Mynydd Rhiw, and they were attracted to the old manor house on its land.

The story has often been told of how the other three sent off a telegram to Honora, asking her 'Will you invest

27

savings in Plas?' to which she replied 'Yes, but haven't got much'. They had already consulted their friend, Clough Williams-Ellis, who had pronounced the roof sound. Their acquaintance with the difficulties involved in property-owning would have dictated this practical step, but it is equally typical they should not have risked their income by selling shares or property in Nottingham.

By the spring of 1939, the purchase had been completed and their builder in Nottingham, F.H. Lambert, was commissioned to make the house habitable. There was much to do. Though the roof was sound, water had entered the ground floor, and when it rained, a continuous stream flowed in through the back door and out through the front. This had to be diverted, the plumbing overhauled (doubtless much of it 'beyond repair') and a coke boiler installed in the old kitchen to heat the house. The work did not go entirely smoothly and Eileen had to write a letter of complaint to Mr Lambert. Yet despite all these difficulties and several illnesses the three ladies moved into the Plas as soon as they could and lived among the alterations, which could not have improved their health.

In the outside world, the rumours of war gathered. Honora wrote to Mr Lambert on the 14th July, hoping he could fulfil his contract. The Keatings were anxious about the completion of the work, as they intended to offer the house as a convalescent home. Whether it was turned down, or whether they thought better of it is unknown. Instead they continued to live at the Plas and on the 22nd August, 1939, Pickfords sent them an invoice for the removal of their furniture from 14 Cranmer Street to Rhiw. The die was cast. It was from Plas yn Rhiw that they coped with all their wartime difficulties, both there and in Nottingham.

Chapter IV

The Inter-War Years – Honora

In 1919, the Women's Land Army was disbanded and Honora's job of Welfare Officer came to an end. Her future was uncertain. An enigmatic inscription in a book in the Plas points to a romantic affair and a conventional role as housewife and mother. Mrs Keating wrote, 'To Honora and Michael' and the date was 1919. None of the documents in the archive tell how the friendship ended, but however it may have been, it must have ended sadly for Honora.

Perhaps it was this which led her to embrace a new career and enrol in King's College of Household and Social Science as a student of midwifery. She completed the course in two years, and then in 1923 came a post which was to afford her the opportunity of influencing the development of child-care throughout Britain in the inter-war years and into the early years of World War II.

Among the side-effects of modern wars has been the perception that the nation lacked sufficient numbers of fit, adequately-educated young men to supply the needs of the armed services. It had been so in the Boer War, it was to be so in World War II, and especially was it so in World

War I, with its insatiable demand for soldiers to fill the places of those who fell in the trenches. A large proportion of the men of military age failed to meet the medical criteria, and after the war various bodies were set up to deal with the problem. Fitness depends on good nutrition and upbringing in infancy. It was recognised that the basis of the solution must be sought in infancy. One of the organisations dealing with this was the Steade Infant Welfare Fund. In 1924, funds were transferred to the Central Council for Infant and Child Welfare for the setting up of a Travelling Exhibition, and placed in the hands of the official Trustees and Charities. Managing Trustees were appointed – Mr H.T. Baker, Warden of Winchester College, Miss Margaret Horn and Lady Cynthia Colville, Woman of the Bedchamber to the Queen. To these Honora applied for the post of Organising Secretary and was duly appointed.

Her duties were primarily aimed at instructing mothers in the care of their children. To this end, there was the Travelling Exhibition, which had to be set up, maintained and, as the name implies, sent out to various venues. Here Honora would meet the mothers and give lectures and demonstrations. As adjuncts to these, she drew up diet sheets suitable for infants and toddlers of various ages. There were also lists of clothing suitable to the different stages of childhood, in each of which Honora insisted that clothing should hang from the shoulders, and not constrict the waist. Later she was to develop knitting and sewing patterns for suitable clothing and engage a woman to design them and cut them out.

As secretary to the Travelling Exhibition, Honora had to report to the Trustees, and especially to present the accounts to the Treasurer, Mr Baker, who had to place them before the Official Trustees of Charities. The arrangements for the meeting of the Trustees were in her hands, and this was no simple matter. Meetings had to take place when Mr Baker was up in London, and when Lady Cynthia was not on one of her tours of duties in attendance on the Queen.

With the passing years, Honora's interests developed. In 1932, the Old Student's Handbook of her former college gave the news that she was responsible for the Maternity and Child Welfare Section of the Museum of the London School of Hygiene and Tropical Medicine. In 1935, she directed two films on infant management for the National Council for Mothers and Child Welfare. On 18th November, Queen Mary, now Queen Mother, visited the Council at Carnegie House, no doubt because of Lady Cynthia's involvement. Among other films she saw the two made by Honora, who was present on the occasion, which was not reported in the press, as the Queen, 'did not wish it'. In 1938, she gave a lecture entitled, 'Methods of Health Education' at a College of Nursing Special Course. She was beginning to be recognised as an expert in her field.

Fresh air was increasingly seen in the inter-war years as necessary to the health of children. In towns and cities where blocks of flats were built for the working-classes, they would be equipped with flat roofs or balconies so that babies could be put out in the air. Where these facilities were non-existent, Honora devised a cage which could be hung outside a window, to hold a baby. This was highly commended by Gwen St Aubyn in the *Times*

Educational Supplement in late 1936, and as late as the Festival of Britain, the architects of the Homes Pavilion planned to include it in their exhibition.

Her work was extended abroad. She took the Travelling Exhibition to Paris and to Amsterdam in 1938. In a letter to her mother from that city she described walking along the canal, and declared that she could eat anything. Here, perhaps, was a hint of the digestive trouble which was to dog her later life – a result of stress and anxiety.

However, her life was not all work. There were holidays – in Nottingham, among her friends and relations – and in Llŷn, which she was beginning to love as her second home, with her mother and sisters and friends who came to stay. Other holidays were taken abroad. At first she joined Eileen and Lorna in Brittany, where their friends looked forward to seeing the three 'misses'. Later she had a holiday in Florence, as witnessed by a brochure from the Hotel Metropole and an Italian museum ticket.

During her holidays she painted water-colour scenes from Llŷn and one of an olive-grove twisted by wind. She exhibited from time to time, including a share of an exhibition in London at the Riviera Studios, where several of her paintings were sold. Other paintings were exhibited in the Midlands and Australia. Some of her work now hangs on the staircase in the Plas, showing the predominant colours of blue and beige-yellow that were fashionable in the twenties and thirties.

London itself provided many diversions – plays, operas, concerts, galleries. One letter describes skating in

Regent's Park and tea with 'Murphy' – Agnes Maud – an old and intimate friend. Sometimes she visited relatives such as her cousins in Deal, who wrote favourably to her mother.

Outside London she would combine pleasure with work. One of her letters describes a long walk on a free Sunday in Scotland, walking the hills and coming down for a good tea at 2d. Sometimes she stayed with friends when she was travelling, for the Keatings had a gift for making friends of the people with whom they came into contact.

Through all this activity, Honora kept in close touch with her family. She wrote to them regularly, describing her activities and seeking to help with their problems. Often she drafted business letters for Eileen. Once she sent an envelope marked, 'Phelebitis cure – Valuable' and another time she sent a cutting about infra-red apparatus.

Later she wrote that she was recuperating in her flat and possibly at this time enquiring about wheels for a bed, which was to become a familiar sight in the district when the daughters pushed their mother along the lanes to enjoy the fresh air, the flowers and scenes she loved. In another letter she wrote from Painswick, looking forward to a month in Rhiw, but hoping she wouldn't be too much for Lorna. Next day she wrote again, mentioning the snowdrops, hoping that the 'morning room' was finished and looking forward to celebrating Easter.

Nineteen thirty nine was to be a momentous year for Honora, but it began badly with the death of her great friend, Agnes Maud Murphy at her home in Painswick, Gloucestershire. Honora spent some time with her there, and afterwards did most of what was necessary to clear up. She paid someone to tend the grave and headstone; she also paid rent and rates and probably cleared out her friend's furniture, having it sent first to London and then to Rhiw. But in March she was so ill that she wrote to Eileen on the 2nd of April that she had a nurse and someone to cook and clean.

Then came the royal recognition of her work, with the award of the OBE. Friends wrote to her with their congratulations and her mother proudly announced it in the local paper. But Honora was not able to go to the Palace for investiture at the first opportunity.

Instead, she was on the high seas, enjoying a cruise arranged by Thomas Cook, on a small cargo boat which carried passengers, the *Glenfinlas*, which left Glasgow on the 15th of April. Her employers had awarded her this holiday as their appreciation of the work she had done for them over the years. At first, because of the rumours of war, she was reluctant to go, but her cousin Edith, among others, persuaded her that there was no likelihood of war.

Her intended destination was the Far East, especially Japan, whose painting techniques she was eager to study. As ever she wrote home frequently – long letters as on 11th June describing the sights she had seen and the places she had visited, such as Fuji and other beauty spots in Japan. Possibly she purchased the print which now hangs in the second floor bedroom.

In the same letter she also mentions the fireplaces of Plas, and stripping them to plain stone. She sketched a typical Welsh fireplace 'as in the laundry'. On 4th July, she wrote to her mother from the Indian Ocean, describing her visit to Penang, and looking forward to Colombo, Suez and Port Said. She expected to be in London on 29th July.

Meanwhile she was reading Howard Spring's 'latest novel' and thinking of 'the shed and the gate' at home being 'done'.

Once home, she took over the planning and planting of the garden. Early in the year she had mentioned the snowdrops which clothe the woods above the house. Now she sent for catalogues such as Waterers, and Pennell's and Murrell's and set about planting dahlias, roses and bulbs. In London, she started organising herself, colleagues and an array of woman volunteers to take care of children in wartime.

Chapter V

War and its aftermath
at Plas yn Rhiw

Settling in at Plas yn Rhiw was greatly complicated by the
outbreak of war in September 1939. Honora, who had only
just managed to reach home in July from her round-the-
world voyage, was urgently needed in London for special
war work, so Eileen and Lorna had to cope on their own
with the difficulties.

Some of them were the same as before. Eileen had to
make numerous visits to Nottingham to see to the
property – visit solicitors, collect rents, give instructions
about repairs and renovations. Also she visited relations,
such as Aunt Emma Keating, who was now living at The
Orchard, Caythorpe. Auntie Pop (Mrs Cropper) had
moved back to Nottingham to live in 1938, after donating
a Hammond organ to the church in Falmouth where she
worshipped. She, too, had to be made much of, and
numerous cousins and friends all claimed her attention.

At home, there was the usual housekeeping, as well as
the planning of the decorations and alterations in the
house. At least once, Honora sent them a sketch labelled

'bedroom' and suggested that the wallpaper should be from Lines which she liked. The gardens, divided into small square plots by low box hedges, required much attention. They 'dug for Victory' by growing vegetables here and in the small vegetable plot at the side of the house. They felt that this was their contribution to the war effort, as their fields were too steep and stony for ploughing. Unfortunately the County War Agricultural Executive Committee did not agree with them and later there were altercations between them.

Whether it was their inexperience or a certain tendency to collective paranoia, they made more difficulties for themselves by believing that someone was poisoning their trees. They even consulted the Department of Botany at Bangor, but most probably the trees were dying of old age and neglect. Later they came to believe that an 'enemy' was responsible for poisoning their beautiful species magnolia, when late frost had caught it buds.

As soon as they had bought the Plas, the Keatings set about adding to their property. They bought Sarn cottage, adjoining their woodlands at the bottom of the hill, which at the time was almost derelict. Its annual rent was £2.10.0. This set the pattern for further acquisitions over the years, so that here they built up another empire, similar to the one they had held sway over in Nottingham. This they were used to; they understood it, it was the family business.

From the first settling in they exercised accustomed hospitality. A grocer's bill of 1940 includes items such as six sponge rolls and six sandwiches. This, too, became almost a 'business' later on, when they entertained in order to gain members for the National Trust.

All this took its toll on Eileen, who had, in addition to the administration of both estates, to help look after Mrs Keating. Many a day the daughters were seen pushing her up the steep hill-sides on the 'bedstead on wheels' which Honora had contrived. One day, they unfortunately let go and the contraption ran out of control, pitching out the old lady, so that she broke her arm. This meant more worry and nursing for them.

As a result of all this, Eileen became ill towards the end of 1939 and had to take to her bed with arthritis. The local doctor was called, and by April of the following year, she was feeling much better, and ascribing her recovery to Sanatogen, prescribed by Honora. May and June saw her back in Nottingham, receiving diathermy treatment. By the end of June she declared herself 'very much better' and had decided to add to her activities by collecting the rents herself, rather than leaving it to the solicitors. Thus began a system whereby relatives or friends, such as Hilda Torrs, or 'Lulu' collected from the tenants and sent the money by post to Rhiw. From time to time, when she was in Nottingham, Eileen would call on the tenants, listen to their complaints and sort out their quarrels. Hers, too, was the last word on who should be granted a tenancy, though she accepted recommendations from her 'collectors' and other tenants.

Until April 1940, the war had not directly touched the Keatings, but with the fall of France and the Battle of Britain, came fears for Honora's safety in London. Each night she sent an anxiously awaited telegram to say she was safe, but others of their friends were not so lucky. Eileen's friend, May Sykes, wrote of being bombed out of her home in Camberwell, and Teresa Holey, too sent bad news. Cousins in Deal complained of nightly raids, but in November there was something of an anti-climax in Teresa's letter from near Hereford, describing how seven sheep had been killed in a neighbouring field.

Nineteen-forty-one brought a terribly cold winter to Britain as a whole, and Llŷn, for once, was no exception. Eileen told her solicitors in Nottingham that she couldn't get to the post-box, because the snow was eighteen feet deep. Buses were unable to run and bread had to be carried in sacks across the field. Yet in January of this year, Eileen agreed to let the cottage in the grounds to the wife and children of a friend, so that they could be away from the bombing. No wonder they didn't stay long. She tried again with a tenant from Nottingham, who complained about the poor quality of the coal. This lady, again, could not have stayed long, because when they heard a programme on the wireless describing the plight of Channel Islanders who'd fled to Britain, they offered it to one of these families, asking for produce in lieu of rent. There is no evidence that the offer was ever taken up, even though she emphasised the similarity of the climate.

Food rationing became even tighter, but despite this, the Keatings sent parcels of butter and lard to their relatives in Nottingham. Another recipient was Eileen's Spanish friend, Carlita, to whom she was able to send a parcel through the League of Nations.

Like other families, the Keatings had evacuees billeted on them, one from Liverpool, called Margaret, and another from London, called Nancy. Margaret and the Keatings seem to have hit it off from the beginning. She called them her 'aunties' and they became friends not only of Margaret herself, but of her sister, Rose, and her mother,

Mrs Hodson, and later Margaret's own daughter, who would visit the Plas on her holidays in northern Wales. She must have been a very perceptive child, because in one of her letters she remarked that although 'auntie Honora' was often bossy and lost her temper with her sisters, she didn't mean it and loved them dearly. Nevertheless she returned to Liverpool in 1942, although the Keatings felt she would regret this.

Nancy was a different matter. In a letter to Eileen in June 1943, Honora begged her sister to come home and deal with the girl, who, she said was sulking and lying. In March, she had returned to London to have her appendix removed, but had come back to Plas, and Honora was intending to take her to Botwnnog, about four miles away, to be signed up for school. She had obviously got under Honora's skin, for a friend staying with Teresa Hooley replying to a letter, described the girl as 'a little perisher'.

Teresa herself was married by this time, but her husband was away in the RAF, working for his commission as a flying officer. They were living in Somerset and the friend described seeing the barrage balloons over Barry. Teresa herself was still writing poetry and giving readings locally, as she had done in Nottingham and the friend said she was 'happy and successful'. Unfortunately, the marriage did not last, and before the divorce in 1943 Teresa was to write that it would be 'a good thing if he were to break his neck'.

In February 1943, the electricity authority wrote asking for way-leave to government installations at Aberdaron, for cables over Plas land, at the far end of the Llŷn peninsula. The Keatings were quite willing, as long as the cables were put underground, so as not to impinge on the beauty of the environment. The electricity company was unwilling to comply, as it was much cheaper to lay overhead cables and at that time neither the beauty of the environment, nor their vulnerability to atomic welfare was a consideration. The Keatings persisted until they were threatened with being reported, as the installations at Aberdaron were involved in the coastal defences. The Plas, at this time, did not have electricity.

Another battle between the Keatings and the authorities concerned the County War Agricultural Executive Committee. They were forced to plough some of their land to grow oats, but the harvest, as they predicted, was meagre. In a grand gesture, they wrote to the Minister of Food, but his reply was suitably diplomatic. He couldn't accept the oats, and advised them to sell it and donate the money to the Red Cross. Nevertheless, they received a bill for harvesting the crop from the 'War Ag' which they were reluctant to pay, so that the War Ag had to send several reminders. When they sent a bill in November, for the services of Italian prisoners from the camp about two miles away, the Keatings, with sweet reason, pointed out that they hadn't asked for the Italians! Among the archives are copies of the War Ag form, which should have given an account of the crops from 1942-1945, but had not been returned. In April 1944, Eileen wrote that there was no point in sending in the forms, as the ground was unsuitable for tilling, citing the disastrous crop of oats. The War Ag's reply was a new bill for ploughing grass.

Another cause of friction with the War Ag was the prevalence of rabbits on Plas land. A few days after the bill for grass ploughing came an order to destroy rabbits. The generally accepted method at the time was gin traps, but in some quarters this was already regarded as causing unnecessary suffering to the animals. Mrs Keating herself replied that gassing should be used. The War Ag was not impressed, the land was not suitable for gas. The Keatings engaged a man to do the gassing but in the end he was unable to come. The Keatings compromised by buying a gun, a gun licence and cartridges.

Co-incidentally, a man appeared on the scene, offering himself as handyman and gamekeeper. This was D.O. Jones, an ex-coastguard, who was looking for work and was willing to shoot the rabbits. Unfortunately he found that he didn't like using the gun, and eventually it was sold to a friend of the Keatings, Mrs Bickford, who was by now occupying Sarn cottage. Probably the rabbits were trapped in the end, because the War Ag wrote to the Keatings twice, urging them to cash a cheque for the rabbits. They would not profit from animal suffering.

As the War drew to an end, Mrs Keating grew gradually weaker and could no longer leave the house, even on the improvised carriage, but her spirit remained buoyant. Margaret's mother, who had been at Plas for a holiday, described her as sitting up in bed, 'singing hymns to the wireless'. Nevertheless, Eileen, on whom the brunt of the nursing fell, declared to her solicitors that she was too exhausted to be able to attend to the business of insuring her handyman and his gun. Then, at the end of January in the middle of a very cold spell, her mother died.

The roads were blocked with snow, and the coffin had to be manhandled across the fields to the little stone-built church of Llanfaelrhys, in whose churchyard she was buried, as were her daughters in their turn. On the journey, a flight of birds passed over the funeral procession, and the daughters had the coffin lid opened so that she could see for the last time the wild creatures she had loved. Over the grave they placed a natural stone with the inscription carved into it.

Peace brought a postcard from Colette, all she was allowed to send, saying that all was well. But the War hadn't quite finished with the Plas. On 16th of September, a land-mine, probably jettisoned by a returning German bomber, exploded on Cilan, the headland forming the eastern arm of the bay. The resulting damage to the Plas was reason enough for a claim to the War Damage Commission.

In other ways, too, the beginning of peace was a sad and dreary time at the Plas. Two other members of the older generation died at this time – Aunt Bertha at The Orchard, Caythorpe, in 1945 and cousin Maud, whose death was relayed to them by Auntie Pop, in 1946. By the end of this year both Honora and Lorna were seriously ill. The War Ag was still pursuing Eileen for the debt which she had thought cancelled. One of the Plas fields was flooded. From Liverpool, Mrs Hodson wrote of the coal shortage, coupons for wool, and the housing shortage which had resulted in her son and daughter both having to live with their in-laws; there were queues for fruit and bread rationing; she was thankful to the Keatings for the margarine, lard and tinned soup (on 'points') which they were able to send her. The Plas estate itself was threatened by the Board of Trade, which wanted to cut down the Bluebell Wood for timber.

Nevertheless, there were the stirrings of the new life

which was to follow. In April, Eileen was able to defend the Bluebell Wood by informing the Board of Trade that the property was being conveyed to the National Trust. On the 2nd of March, 1947, their solicitor wrote to them to say that the Deed of Gift was ready for execution. A new era was starting.

The garden was taking shape; new plants were being bought and seeds sown, though occasionally the seed packet was forgotten and left neglected for the next fifty years. But the Zéphirine Drouhin roses, trained up the pillars of the verandah were to sweeten the air around the front door for the next half century. This was chiefly Honora's province, and early in 1947, Honora came home to them, this time for good. From then on the three sisters lived and worked together to promote the Plas as a National Trust property and to defend their beloved Llŷn.

Among their friends, Teresa Hooley published her selected poems, with the publisher Jonathan Cape. Her domestic affairs were not going well, however. She was unsettled and as a result of one house-move, she sent a stove to the Plas as a gift and a gramophone as a loan. Their handyman, D.O. Jones, became ill, had to go to hospital and left. His new work took him to Ireland, where he had 'a pal in the police' who obtained unrationed chocolates for him to send to his former employers.

At the end of the year Lorna was ill again, probably with gall bladder trouble. Honora accompanied her to Liverpool, where she was operated on by Howell Hughes. Honora heartily wished there was a phone at the Plas, but she found time to attend a concert of the Liverpool Philharmonic Orchestra. As usual, Lorna made many friends at the nursing home and continued to correspond with them long after she returned home.

Chapter VI

Honora's War Work – London

Shortly before she went on her round-the-world voyage, Honora had become involved in plans for dealing with children evacuated from their homes and thus separated from their parents, should the Damoclean sword fall and the impending war become a reality. Organisations beside the Infant Welfare Fund were already drawing up contingency plans, notably the WVS, who has plans for Civil Defence, and the Women's Group on Public Welfare, who nominated Honora as a member of their Emergency Committee. Her response was to put forward suggestions for a Child Care Corps, to help with the billeted children.

When she returned to work in September, she set about organising this body of women, who would be trained in child welfare, and able to take charge of Day Nurseries for the under-fives. This involved certification, which meant that the members of the Child Care Corps would have to be examined, which in turn meant that they would have to follow a set syllabus, for which lecturers would have to be found. Honora threw herself into the work with her usual enthusiasm, drawing up syllabuses, framing model exam questions, using her contacts to find lecturers, and contributing to a handbook for members.

In the meantime, her ordinary work went on – travelling with the Exhibition, giving lectures, organising meetings of the Trustees of the Institute of Infant Welfare Fund, and attending endless committee meetings. One fruit of her labours was 'A Scheme for the Provision of Extra Clothing and Nursery Equipment for the Children Under Five Years Old'. Here she showed how nursery equipment and toys could be devised from boxes and waste material. A fortunate discovery enabled her to buy £50 worth of flannel for making children's clothing, though a telegram to the Treasurer of the IIWF asking permission had to be followed up by a letter to explain her thinking behind the purchases. Her next move was to set up working parties to make up patterns for the garments – an activity which was to grow and have repercussions as the war developed.

This routine was pleasantly interrupted in February 1940, by two royal occasions. One was the investiture, deferred for nearly a year, when she received her OBE. Unfortunately, neither of her sisters was able to accompany her to the Palace, but she wrote them a full account afterwards. The second was a visit by the Queen to her office, to see the Exhibition for herself. A story which probably appertains to this occasion sounds typical enough of Honora to be true. She informed her Majesty that oatmeal was good for children, and that she should see to it that her little girls had porridge for breakfast. When the Queen replied that they didn't like porridge, Honora suggested oatcakes.

As always, her family was constantly in her thoughts. Every night she sent them a telegram to tell them that she

The house before the removal of the plaster.

Entrance Hall will door open showing downstairs 'parlour' (2000).

49

Magnolia Campbellii Mollicomata with Porth Neigwl and Cilan headland in the background.

The cottage, previously laundry (August 1994)

Road down from Plas with Bryn Ffoulk on right.

Panshanger – the grounds.

Honora (centre) with some of her 'family at Panshanger.

Honora with two of her 'children'

*Eileen and Meg at her seat
(copyright Wester Mail)*

Eileen, Honora and Lorna with Mildred Eldrigde (Mrs. R.S. Thomas) taken by Min Ottley, September 1965.

Honora and Lorna in the garden.

Eileen (seated) with Lorna and Honora gathering roses
(written at the side 'roses three of us')

Eileen's seat, August 1994

Honora, Eileen and Lorna in the garden with Meg (taken 3 weeks before Eileen's death) (copyright Western Mail)

Honora at Penrhyn Castle, with Mr. & Mrs. Hywel D. Roberts and Mr. & Mrs. Vincent Morgan of the Caernarfonshire sub-committee of the CPRW. (copyright: Liverpool Daily Post)

Churchyard at Llanfaelrhys:
headstone on grave of
Mrs Constance Annie Keating.

Churchyard at Llanfaelrhys:
flat, rustic stone over grave of the
Keating sisters.

Churchyard at Llanfaelrhys where the women of Plas yn Rhiw are buried
(one of the churches in R.S. Thomas' care).

was safe. She looked for wallpapers for the Plas from firms such as Sanderson and Lines, but suggested in a letter to Lorna in April that as prices were rising so quickly they should purchase the paint through their decorator to take advantage of wholesale prices. For the garden she sent for nurserymen's catalogues and received among others Waterer's Spring Catalogue for their sale of herbaceous and Alpine plants, and Ramsbottom and Co's flower catalogue. In her letters she told Lorna and Eileen what needed doing in the garden.

By the time of the Fall of France and Dunkirk the syllabus for the Child Care Reserve was complete, and Lady Galway sent out a circular letter concerning it to Medical Officers of Health throughout the country. The response was slow, but by September, when the blitz began, replies began to come in from such places as Newcastle, Harrogate, Wrexham, Manchester, Leeds, Dewsbury, Warrington and Cardiff. Some were merely asking for further details, but Manchester and Warrington were interested in setting up courses, and from Manchester came a request for a draft prospectus and syllabus.

In the midst of all this activity, Honora became ill. On 25th September, the same day as she received a report from the Nursery Leader of a hostel for evacuees from Gibraltar, which she was overseeing, she returned home to be nursed by her sisters. Her colleague, Mabel Dowden, wrote soon after to report that the Queen's Theatre had been gutted, and hoping that she'd arrived safely.

At first, she expected to make a speedy recovery and return to work. She was constantly in touch with her office, mainly through Mabel Dowden, who informed her of matters such as the Women's Group for Public Welfare sending a list of names of members who'd be prepared to receive evacuees from 'non-target' areas; stating that her salary was being sent; that Lady Galway's home, Cromwell House, had been bombed, that *Mother and Child* and *Nursing Mirror* wanted to publish her notes. Lady Galway herself wrote firstly on 30th September, to say she was glad that Honora was being looked after and again on 15th October, glad that she was better, but warning her not to come back too soon, as the staff knew what to do.

Another correspondent was Zoe Puxley, from the Ministry of Health, who had been in touch with Mr Armer of the Welsh Board of Health concerning Day Nurseries. He'd informed Miss Puxley that there was no difficulty with female labour in Wales. Honora went ahead, arranging an interview with the Town Clerk of Wrexham and contacting Olive Wheeler, Professor of Education in Cardiff. In the outcome, she was not able to visit either.

As September rolled into October, the response to another appeal of Honora's became apparent. Mabel Howden reported that the office had received a number of dolls, in response to an appeal in *House and Country*. E.B. Haynes described a number of toys received in response to an article in the WI magazine. Even J.B. Priestly, whose wife was starting a Day Nursery for evacuees, made a broadcast appeal for toys and dolls. The Day Nurseries were being equipped, not merely with boxes and waste materials. The London County Council Homes for Lost Children wrote to say that member of the Child Care Reserve were doing marvellous work.

On the 4th November, Zoe Puxley wrote that there was a branch of the Child Care Reserve established at

Manchester. She wondered if Honora would be arranging exams for the Civil Nursing Reserve, as she was glad to hear that she expected to be fit soon. But Honora was far from fit. The illness had affected her lung; recovery would be long and slow. Already Lady Galway was pressing her to send in medical certificates to cover her absence from work, but Honora appeared reluctant to do so.

By December, her life was running on two levels. On the one hand, she was working on an article for the Women's Gas Council, which she managed to deliver by the end of the month. On the other, she was beginning to realise that her illness would be lengthier than she had at first visualised. Miss Moffat, the secretary to the NCMCW, wrote on the 17th about salary arrangements while she was ill, but accepted that there was no question of TB, which at that time would almost automatically have meant that she would not have been able to return to her demanding job. Dame Louise McElroy wrote a friendly letter ostensibly looking forward to seeing her back, but possibly making an enquiry as to how she felt about returning. Finally, on 31st December came a request from the Central Council for Health Education for lecturers in Underground shelters – the last place for someone with a dubious lung. On top of this, the buildings (in Camden Town) which housed Honora had been hit twice, once in early November, and again in December. This time it was unsuitable for occupation for nine days. Later, a friend who'd been out of London for two years, found a blackened building and was told that Honora had gone to Wales 'for the duration'.

By January, it was clear to the committee which ran NCMCW, that Honora had finished her career with them.

In January 1941, Honora wrote to her friend, Lady Janet Forber, complaining that the Committee had written directly to her GP. She described the financial difficulties of her family and herself, saying she would like to work in Wales, which she felt was backward and primitive compared to Malaya, which she'd visited on her voyage. She declared that she couldn't work in underground shelters, but could travel. Since she'd caught her 'flu germ' at work, she wondered if she could sue for compensation, as for an accident; she could work on the land, as she'd done in World War I. Should she go to the Exhibitions Committee?

In reply, Lady Forber explained the need for a consultant's report and reminded her of the need to send in ordinary medical certificates. She thought there might well be work for her in Liverpool or Manchester. She begged Honora not to write and say she was wrong, nor to go to the Committee.

The upshot was that on the 6th of March, the secretary of the Exhibitions Committee wrote expressing the regrets of the Committee that Honora had to take a year off for her health, and thanking her for her work for them. This was followed on the 21st by a statement of her financial position: her salary from March to December of 1940 was £272.13.9, made up partly of full-salary and partly of half-salary. A suggestion, mooted by Margaret Horn, that she should be given a maintenance grant of £150 for the year was later adopted. As from the 1st of January 1941, Honora was no longer the Organiser of the Travelling Exhibitions.

A bitter blow, but at home at the Plas, Honora was already looking to the future. One of her first acts was to buy a pair of boots, presumably for 'working on the land'. When she approached Clark's of Glastonbury they couldn't supply her and warned her there was a shortage, but suggested Harrods. In keeping with their reputation, they were able to send her a pair – at £3.9.3 – a princely sum! There was plenty of work in the garden and in the house, for Mrs Keating was sinking slowly and required more and more attention. Honora helped Eileen with business affairs, drafting letters for her sisters to write and dealing with some, such as the Inland Revenue, in her own name. It was she who arranged for the 'family from Liverpool' – the wife and children of an acquaintance of hers – to occupy the cottage. In her leisure time she painted in the little parlour on the ground floor.

All this did not fully use up her restless energy. On the 1st of April, she gave a talk to Pwllheli WI, together with her friend, Dr Richards or 'Dickie', whom she had been instrumental in bringing to Tyn y Coed, a farm at the foot of Mynydd Rhiw. She gave a talk to the Caernarfonshire County Nursing Association. The secretary had to warn her that her audience's children were 'grown-up'. She must have impressed Pwllheli WI, as the secretary asked her to speak to a resolution on evacuees. Here she could speak from the heart! Nearer home, a 'Health Talk' was billed for the Botwnnog WI, by Miss Honora Keating, OBE, for 21st July.

In June, Honora received a letter from Margaret Horn, one of the Trustees of the Institute of Infant Welfare Fund, looking to the future. She begged Honora not to go back to her old job, as the 'atmosphere' there would wear her out. Instead, she advised her to seek a job in a Government Department, ready for post-war reconstruction. In asking after her lung, she warned her not to speak in crowded halls!

The advice about not returning to her old job was superfluous. Honora had already given up the tenancy of her flat and was arranging for the removal of boxes of her possessions. Nor was she in a position to consider another post. After Mabel Dowding visited her in July, she reported that her health was still not good. This elicited Lady Galway's sympathy, but no suggestion for the future. By August, the details of moving-out were complete. Honora recognised that no-one would want a flat in Lambeth at that time, as her correspondents were constantly mentioning bombs.

The end of the year came and went, and with it the end of Honora's maintenance grant. She still retained an interest in the Exhibitions, and her employers were anxious not to sever their connection with her. At a meeting of the Exhibitions Sub-Committee on the 17th of June, 1942, it was passed that she should be retained as Honorary Consultant, without salary, but with grants for any special requirements. A new member of staff had been appointed, and Margaret Horn was made responsible for new patterns and model garments for the Mother and Child Welfare Conference, but Honora would be still a member of the Committee, and would be consulted for baby clothes. In December, Miss Horn, writing to Honora, said she should be in charge of Wales, probably meaning the Child Care Reserve, but when she did find another job, it was to be quite different from anything she had tackled before.

In the meantime, several rows broke out at the NCMCW. One concerned the future of the Permanent

Exhibition. Miss Horn had fears about this and thought the Board of Education the proper body for its educational work. She told Honora she'd written to Lady Cynthia Colville explaining this. Lady Cynthia disagreed. She thought it might go under Health, rather than Education. Honora wrote back, saying the Exhibition be moved to a safe place for the duration, and suggesting the Ministry of Health. Yet another destination was put forward by Dr Mary Ormsby, after reading an article in *The Spectator* or by Dame Georgina Butler. She thought it would be well to co-ordinate knowledge of courses for the Disabled and others at the Central Bureau of Information. None of these ladies wrote as though she foresaw the war continuing for another two years, but an interesting echo of World War I came in a letter from Dame Louise McElroy, showing how 'ignorant mothers' and the scandals brought to light by evacuation showed the need for the Exhibitions to continue.

Another row concerned the patterns themselves. It was almost inevitable that Honora should be accused of interfering in the work, and the person employed to do the designing appealed to Margaret Horn, who subsequently wrote that she was 'very pleased' with the work and that the cutter was 'loyal'. Honora was well off out of this 'atmosphere'. Still, when Lady Cynthia found she couldn't spare time to serve on an Adoption Committee of the 'National Council for the Unmarried Mother and her Child', Honora nominated Miss Horn in her place.

Despite this, the work went on, with Honora using her artistic skill to design a block for printing on the envelopes containing the patterns, and continuing to correspond with the Treasurer of the Infant Welfare Fund.

It was gratifying too, when the Central Council for Health Education showed an interest in her films. She was able to respond with an account of five films and their intended audiences.

All this changed suddenly, in August, when Honora was appointed to an entirely new job – Matron of Panshanger in Hertfordshire, a hostel for pregnant servicewomen run by the Ministry of Health. Here she found a new vocation at the age of forty-seven.

Chapter VII

Honora's War Work – Panshanger

'This is the most useful work I think I have been able to do.' Honora was writing from Panshanger to the Warden of Winchester towards the end of 1945. She had been Matron for over two years, and, as always, had thrown her heart and soul into the work. She was well suited to it, having worked theoretically with mothers and babies for over twenty years. It was well suited to her, for here she was in sole charge and could exercise a kindly despotism over girls and staff.

Panshanger was a large house near Hertford, the home of William Henry Grenfall, first Baron Desborough of Taplow, who died in 1945 at the age of ninety, and Lady Desborough. When Honora arrived in July 1943, the Desboroughs had moved out, having no heir, as both their sons had been killed in World War I. Lady Desborough was living near enough to take a close interest in the house and its new inhabitants. It was large enough to take forty girls at a time, together with twenty-one babies.

The routine was for pregnant service-women to be referred by the welfare officers of their service and to spend between three and four months at the hostel, usually half the time before the birth and half after. Soon after admission they were sent to a hospital in Great Cozens or the Hertfordshire County Hospital, for a check-up.

This routine was often varied. Occasionally there would be an outbreak of infectious disease among the girls. Once it was scarlet fever and the sufferer had to be removed to an isolation hospital, while swabs were taken and the sick girls kept in isolation. Even the doctor was in quarantine. Sadly, a baby would sometimes die, and it fell to Honora to arrange and attend a funeral service in accordance with the mother's religion.

By contrast, weddings were happy occasions. Honora seems to have had her own methods in bringing them about. Several times in a year a man would arrive to see his girl-friend or fiancé. The next day he would be sent to see the Registrar. Two days after his arrival there would be a wedding at the Registry Office, or occasionally in 'our lovely little village church', at Hertingfordbury. Other visitors were the girls' parents and occasionally their sisters. Sometimes married women were visited by their husbands.

Official visits were paid by Employment Officers, Ministers of Religion, welfare workers and prospective employers. Once a librarian came, but the books which followed were returned after three days.

Less serious activities included socials and Christmas parties. Once there was a summer fete, which raised the sum of £20 towards a small 'Panshanger Fund'. Another time the girls went to help a local farmer harvest his fruit. One Christmas, Lady Desborough invited them to a party, where she entertained them with a conjurer.

On a practical level, there were classes in sewing and cookery, in order to enable girls to provide suitable clothing for their children, and a good, nutritious diet. The girls were also taught the importance of fresh air, with windows being kept open and the girls themselves encouraged to spend time out-of-doors.

Life at Panshanger was as useful and pleasant as Honora could make it for the girls, but eventually they had to leave and face a world which was not kind to single mothers. This was especially true of Irish girls, who were officially looked after by the War Office, and also West Indian and Belgian girls who could be discharged in Great Britain so that their families wouldn't know the reason for their discharge. No wonder that the majority of them chose adoption for their children. A notebook labelled 'Private Adoptions' contained the names of the children and the families adopting them. These seem to have been arranged by Honora herself, through various contacts.

There was no attempt to keep the girls in the dark about who the adopting parents were. Indeed, the new parents once came back to Panshanger with the child, to visit its natural mother. Honora sent a circular letter to adopting parents asking them for photographs of the children at various stages. She wrote back, thanking them for their replies, and sent the news and the photographs on to the mothers if they wanted them. They, in turn, wrote back to thank her, with news of the new lives they were creating for themselves. Rarely was there a rebuff, as when a father wrote back saying he felt his daughter should forget her baby.

On discharge, the girls themselves might go back to their families or to their new husbands, but many had no homes to go to. Often a residential post was found for them as a cook, or as an auxiliary in a hospital, but here a difficulty could arise. They hadn't the money for the fare to their new job and had to be helped by the S.S.H.S. If the job was non-residential, a billeting officer would help them to find lodgings. In extreme cases Honora would take them back at Panshanger, for instance, if they were ill. With one girl, at least, she roused the local police to look for her when she'd failed to find a billet.

The advent of peace made little difference to the routine of life at Panshanger, but clearly there would be an end to its purpose. This came early in 1947, but already, at the end of 1946, it was being run down. Writing to Eileen and Lorna, near Christmas of that year, Honora said she was down to 10 girls, whereas she had at one time had 50 in her care.

The closing of the hostel did not spell the end of her connection with it. At Christmas 1947, she wrote to all the girls who had been at Panshanger while she was Matron. Many of their replies make moving as well as amusing reading. One Irish girl said she nearly made herself ill with cream cakes on landing in her native country. Others sent photographs of their new families or the baby they'd had while at Panshanger. One wrote that she was with the BAOR, 1947, in Germany and found the winter grim. A common dilemma was what to do about the birth certificate, or whether to tell her new fiancé about the child she'd had. Honora answered one such inquirer by telling her to follow her own heart. She continued to follow the careers of some of the girls until as late as 1953.

Honora loved her work at Panshanger and was proud of it. She had received a visit from Queen Mary in 1946, setting the seal of official approval. Nevertheless, it had taken a heavy toll on a constitution already weakened by illness. Early on, she wrote to a friend that she worked from eight in the morning till eleven at night. There would have been much to do: interviewing girls, relatives, officials, staff, arranging births, weddings, funerals, liaising with doctors, nurses, ministers of religion, lawyers, officers of court, adopting parents, visits to London for meetings at the Ministry of Health, plans for small treats for the girls. After all this, there would be endless paperwork, not to mention the odd hitch, as when the cook left and she had to organise girls who'd had experience of cooking to prepare the meals.

In addition to all this, there was unfinished business connected with her old job. By 1943, the majority of the evacuees had returned home, so there was not the pressure to organise the Child Care Reserve. On the other hand, there were hints of trouble among those running the National Council for Mother and Child Welfare. Honora's receipt of the minutes of the meeting of the Exhibitions Sub-Committee held on the 9th September, 1943, suggests that she was still a member of that committee and of the main committee, and would have travelled to London to attend the meetings. It must have been a shock, therefore when her friend, Margaret Horn, resigned from both committees, after resisting pleas, including one from the Vice-Chairman of the Exhibitions Committee, M.W. Perowne. A letter addressed to Miss Horn, from Lord Roxborough, telling her that a solicitor was needed to deal with the designer's claim for a 10% royalty on her patterns, gives a hint of the dispute that may have led to this step. Her fellow trustee of the Institute of Infant

Welfare Fund, H.T. Baker, showed a full understanding of the situation. He wrote that she had acted wisely, because of the troubles at Carnegie House, where the office was.

By the beginning of 1944, this was being run by a new organiser, Mrs A.B. Meering. She wanted to add to the exhibits, and wrote to the Treasurer, H.T. Baker, concerning the financial position of the Exhibitions. Honora as secretary, wrote in turn, to Mrs Meering to tell her that the IIWF wouldn't be able to meet any expenditure by the Committee in 1944. The accountants explained to the Treasurer that payments had been made to Honora in 1942 and 1943, and that by 1944 the Fund had almost exhausted its former surplus. Honora herself wrote to Miss Moffatt, describing expenditure of £24 by the NCMCW for patterns for the IIWF as having been made without her knowledge. Financial complications must have made her feel glad that she was out of the office atmosphere.

Other worries concerned the future of the IIWF and the NCMCW themselves. A proposed merger of the latter with the National Council of Social Services was approved by H.T. Baker. A few days later, Honora, conveyed approval of the Trustees to Miss Moffatt at the NCMCW.

But it was not quite defunct. When the war ended in 1945, Honora attempted to arrange a meeting of the three original Trustees – Lady Cynthia, Margaret Horn and H.T. Baker, to discuss 'the whole position'. Lady Cynthia made 'no reply', Miss Horn asked whether it was extinct and on the 4th November she was forced to report to the Accountants, that she'd been unable to arrange a meeting. Nevertheless Honora persisted and on 23rd drafted letters to Lady Cynthia and Miss Horn, to arrange a meeting. The balance of the fund was then down to £143. By the end of 1944, Mr Baker, frustrated that the Trustees were doing no more than signing cheques, wrote to say that the IIWF was dormant. Nevertheless, Honora kept an account book for it until 1952.

Finances occupied Honora and the Trustees during the early part of 1945. She wrote many letters to the auditors, the charity commissioners and the Trustees. Finally she managed to arrange a meeting for the 25th of July. The main discussion concerned the appointment of Zoe Puxley as a Trustee, on the resignation of Lady Cynthia. This was confirmed in September, when Honora wrote to her officially requesting her to become a Trustee.

Meanwhile, changes were taking place at the NCMCW. Its annual report for 1945 announced that Carnegie House was to be taken over by the Carnegie UK Trust, making the NCMCW homeless. It was offered 48 Queen's Gardens as temporary offices, but the grants from the Carnegie Trust were almost at an end. Despite this, the exhibitions were continuing and being revised and the educational work was being extended into schools. Honora would have noted that her name was not mentioned in any of this. It would not have been any consolation to hear from Margaret Horn in March 1947 that the NAMCWW, with which the MCMCW had been amalgamated, might end in March and that the fate of the exhibitions, which Honora had built up over so many years, was undecided.

Honora had hardly been in her new post at Panshanger for a month, when she wrote home to say that she was coming back for her mother's birthday. Subsequently the Diary records many instances of Matron's return home, sometimes on leave, once on compassionate leave, at the time of her mother's death, and sometimes, more sinisterly, on sick leave. By Christmas 1946, when the hostel was down to ten girls, Honora had to confess to her sisters that she'd been ill, and it was clear that there was something very wrong. In January 1947, she was suffering from her old trouble, bronchitis, and also from her gall-bladder.

In February, she entered the South London Hospital for Women, where she had X-rays for her gall-bladder trouble. She thought that Lorna should go there, too, once the snow had cleared, for she was apparently suffering from the same complaint.

Eventually Honora had her gall-bladder removed at St Saviour's Hospital, and was surprised and alarmed at the amount of pain she suffered. Lorna, who was with her, was extremely anxious about her. She was there for a fortnight.

Panshanger was closed down on 28th February, 1947, but Honora remained there until 25th March. This time she went home for good, although she made several attempts to find a new post. She wrote to Dr Sutherland, Secretary to the Central Council for Health Education, requesting an interview on the strength of her work as organiser at NCMCW for 20 years, but turned down a post as Matron of a Children's Home for which he recommended her. Zoe Puxley wrote of a similar post at a home for homeless children in Chantilly, near Paris, with some teaching included, this also came to nothing. As she wrote to one of her 'girls' she was longing to be back in Rhiw, tending her garden, and there she remained, apart from short absences, for the rest of her life, though she did much more than tend her garden.

At Panshanger, a disastrous fire destroyed the building which had been her temporary home for three and a half years. As there was no heir, the land was sold for development. It was as if it had not existed. Honora could not bear the thought of the same fate overtaking her permanent home at Rhiw: the house which she and her sisters had so lovingly restored; the garden which she had brought to life from the entanglements she had inherited; the snowdrop and bluebell wood above the house; daffodils on the hillside sloping down to the road. She cast around for some means of preserving these to be enjoyed by future generations. The answer seemed to be to donate it to the National Trust. Simple as this solution was, it was hedged about with difficulties. Overcoming them was Honora's primary aim when she left Panshanger, exhausted, sick, seeing the work to which she had devoted twenty years of her life being ably executed without her.

Chapter VIII

Another Panshanger (i)

By May 1948, Honora was contacting the National Trust with proposals for making over the property, while retaining an interest. To her sisters she suggested a settlement which would include giving money in Trust to the National Trust to pay death duties. She was afraid that the survivor might change her mind otherwise. As the youngest, she could expect to be the survivor, but illness had weakened her, and it was little more than a year since she had given up her gruelling post at Panshanger. However, there was much correspondence to be carried on, negotiations to be entered into and formalities to be completed, before the property was finally handed over.

One of the first formalities was the valuation of the house. On the 12th of June this stood at £4,000, with the contents valued at £850 – modest by National Trust standards.

The Memorandum of wishes agreed contained a clause concerning the trapping of rabbits.

The boundaries were mapped, and by May 1949, the conveyance had been drafted, together with that of Mynydd Cilan – the other arm of Porth Neigwl. These were agreed, together with their accompanying engrossments, by the beginning of November, so that by 28th of that month the National Trust was able to inform the Keatings that there would be a description of Plas yn Rhiw in their next list of properties. In their next supplement to the list, Cilan appeared, but not Rhiw. On the 11th February, 1950, *The Times* sealed the transaction in its usual way, publishing a large photograph of the Plas woods white with drifts of snowdrops.

From then on the Keatings became actively involved with the work of the National Trust. The promoted membership by inviting guests to tea. After regaling them with Philadelphia cheese and bought Swiss roll, and showing them round the house and gardens, they invited them to join the Trust. It was difficult to refuse! By September 1951, the secretary was congratulating them on the new members enrolled.

One of the visitors who did not need to be enrolled, as he was already a member, was Sir Compton McKenzie, author of *Whiskey Galore*, who came in the summer of 1950, when he was preparing his book, *I Took a Journey*, which gives details of many Trust properties which he visited. He was more interested in the lunch which the sisters prepared for him than the view – which was shrouded in mist. He had to take their word for it that it was glorious to look across Bae Ceredigion and see the Meirionnydd hills dappled in sunlight. As usual, they made a friend of him and several years later he acknowledged a spray of white heather they sent to him.

Finally on the 15th of July, 1952, the deeds were officially handed over, and the Supplement to the List of Properties published in September included Plas yn Rhiw, while the Report for 1950-52 named the Misses Keating, of Plas-yn-rhiw as benefactors. Sarn cottage, insured at £600, was not included and was to continue to be lent to the Keatings' friends. A legacy of their Nonconformist up-bringing was the clause that the Plas was never to be used for the sale of intoxicating liquor.

The transfer of the Plas to the National Trust meant that repairs and improvements to the fabric of the building had to be put in train. F.W. Armitage, chairman of the National Trust recommended as architect, Colin Gresham of Cricieth. However, although a qualified architect, he had never registered, and the job fell to W.A. Singleton, a lecturer in architecture at Manchester University.

He submitted a preliminary specification for the work early in 1949, and advised them over their claim for War Damage from the land mines which had fallen on Cilan and incidentally damaged the roof. He also advised them on obtaining the licence which was then necessary for £500 worth of building materials. But the builders were slow. By the end of February 1950, they had received a solicitor's letter to terminate their arrangements and remove their tackle. Honora complained about the waterfall wall and flood damage to the wall of the drive. The builders in turn threatened legal action over other work elsewhere for the Keatings. Eileen complained about the size of the bill.

More happily they arranged for the erection of a weather-vane and new gates. Honora suggested they should look for second-hand ones, but eventually they had new ones made in Cricieth. They kept the handle of the old one. Safes were installed and National Trust signs erected, after some argument over their location.

Soon after the National Trust accepted the Plas, another Llŷn property came on the market, the Plas and land at Carreg, near the tip of the peninsula – which they had previously contemplated as a home. Being on its exposed Western side, the coast here is rocky and bare, as opposed to the fertile land to the south-east of Rhiw, but the scenery is breathtaking, especially an almost inaccessible cove called Porth Orion. When they heard of the sale, the Keatings decided this would be a suitable gift to the National Trust, but the secretary, F.W. Armitage was not enthusiastic. He wrote explaining why the Trust might not be able to accept it, even if the Keatings were successful in purchasing it. Nevertheless they went ahead and consulted a local land-agent, who suggested offering £70 for Lot 8 – the land around Porth Orion. The offer was made, the vendors were willing to sell Lot 8 on its own, and on the 7th of November, the purchase was confirmed. One of those who wrote to congratulate them was Colonel Wynne Finch, squire of Cefnamlwch, an estate a little to the east of Carreg. Despite their misgivings, the Trust accepted the gift in April of the following year. Following this success, the sisters contemplated the purchase and donation of Porthor, a neighbouring beach, popular with holiday makers because of its whistling sands. This, however, did not occur during the life-time of any of them.

They were not so fortunate with another purchase – a pair of cottages called Ty'n Llan at Llaniestyn, a secluded village some five miles inland from the Plas. Originally bought about the time of her divorce by Eileen's friend, May Sykes, so that she could be near her friend, they proved unsuitable. A tenant of the Keatings in

Nottingham, who rented a studio from them, wrote in 1948 that he was prepared to buy these cottages. The sale must have fallen through, for later in the year Eileen wrote offering them to the National Trust. After some negotiating, the Trust turned them down despite sketches by Honora, much to Eileen's disappointment.

Soon after, she offered a ten-year lease to their architect W.A. Singleton and F.J. Walker, which was accepted. Mr Singleton set about digging drains, making alterations and decorating. The Keatings were not entirely satisfied with these, resulting in a contretemps over the water-supply. The following year Singleton asked to be released from his agreement, pleading pressure of work as he was now lecturing in the summer vacation. The Keatings consented and kept possession of the cottages, as the National Trust had left the door open for their acceptance after the death of all the sisters.

Meanwhile social life went on at the Plas. The Keatings had kept in touch with their evacuee, Margaret, who had several holidays with them, some with her mother. In 1948 they invited her back to live with them and help them. Margaret came, but stayed only a short time, because she felt that her mother had been upset when she left, and needed her at home. She was troubled because they had given her money and felt she must earn money to repay them, so she took a job in a biscuit factory. Shortly afterwards she announced her engagement, and in April 1951, her mother wrote to say that she was getting married. Soon she was expecting a baby and then another, and moving to a new house. Life was not idyllic, though. Her mother was ill and had to have an operation; her brothers and sisters were jealous of the attention being paid to her by the Keatings. Through all these vicissitudes she wrote to her 'aunties' long, loving letters full of appreciation of what they had done for her and her family. A letter in which she criticises a friend for having too many babies suggests absorption of Honora's teaching.

Older friends were not forgotten, either. May Sykes, no longer interested in a cottage at Llaniestyn, explored the possibility of buying another house in the district, from the Nanhoron estate. This seems to have fallen through and after spending some time at the White House in Abersoch she moved down to Kent, where she spent some time with a cousin of the Keatings, Alice, at Deal, before settling down with her daughter and son-in-law in Bearsted, outside Maidstone. Like Margaret, she wrote long letters about her family and their difficulties, and the Keatings made various offers of help. In return, May (or Margaret or Margaret May, as she variously signed herself) would sew for them, once altering a coat they'd been given, telling Honora it should be ample for her, since she was so 'flat' in front.

Their French friends resumed contact, after the first postcard to say that all was well. In May or June 1949, Colette arranged for her daughter, Nicole, to visit Plas yn Rhiw. Here she met Margaret and was photographed with her. In writing to them the following Christmas she described her life in Paris – mentioning dancing and parties, with people bringing their own food and wine, but her mother said she was unhappy except when she'd been staying at the old family summer haunt of Bréhat. She attempted to send Lorna a bottle of Cognac, but customs would not allow it. Nicole sent a tray-cloth to Margaret in return for help in sending a cake to France.

Their oldest friend, Teresa Hooley, divorced since 1943, had resumed her maiden name, under which she wrote a regular piece for a local Nottingham newspaper. She sent off-prints, in which she mentioned a visit to the Plas, as well as many speaking engagements around Nottingham. Her Christmas gifts to the sisters were annual subscriptions to such periodicals as *Punch*, *The Countryman* and *John O'London's Weekly*. They sent her flowers and fruit from the garden, and received copies of her various books of poems. But after enumerating her faults in letter, Honora concluded, with just a touch of jealousy 'Eileen is her best friend'.

While May Sykes and Teresa Hooley were the main correspondents, there was a whole host of other friends and relatives to be kept up with. One Christmas they received over a hundred cards, not counting gifts and letters. Aunts Emma and Alice (Auntie Pop) were still alive and Eileen visited them when she went over to Nottingham on business. Aunt Emma lived outside the town at Caythorpe and Aunt Alice complained that Eileen paid more attention to Emma, but each received gifts of snowdrops, bluebells in season, lily of the valley and small gifts of butter and lard scraped together from their meagre rations. By 1952, Auntie Pop, too, was beginning to feel her frailty, and realising that her world had changed: the butcher was rude, because she hadn't helped over a flat that the Keatings had to let; taxes were high; she felt it dishonest to take the State Pension; she hadn't seen Lorna for fifty years because she was unable to travel. Various cousins also corresponded – Diana, Gwen, Edith, Alice, 'Carlie' and kept them informed of family events.

While old friends and relatives were kept up with, new

friends were made. A good instance of this was in March 1948, when the County Council proposed to tarmac the drive which passed the house, making it suitable for cars. They had believed that it was a private drive, but the Clerk of the Council, Gwilym T. Jones, argued that it was a public right of way. Though the Keatings had to submit, they invited the Clerk to tea and soon were on a friendly footing with him and his wife, whom they offered a cottage for a holiday. They continued to correspond with his wife even after his death.

Another new friend was the sculptor, Jonah Jones, whose life they saved by sending him to a sanatorium when he had galloping consumption. He acknowledged their kindness by carving the inscription on the stone tablet opposite the gate, noting the gift of the Plas to the National Trust to commemorate the lives of their parents – John William Keating and Constance Annie Keating.

(ii) Honora

Although Honora entered fully into the life of the Plas, and despite further serious illnesses in 1949 and 1951, she continued also to keep an interest in her former activities.

The National Council for Mother and Child Welfare was in financial difficulties, which led to its liquidation in May 1948. Its parent body, the Institute for Infant Welfare Fund was to take over the exhibitions and staff, who were working part-time in other jobs, and in their own homes. Still officially the Secretary to the Trustees, Honora had to liaise with the Trustees, the accountants and the staff. She had also to make arrangements for the safe housing of the exhibitions until they could be permanently disposed of. This she did by putting them into storage at Druce and Co's Depository, a task that was not helped by the fact that some of the furniture as well as some of the exhibitions had been temporarily stored at the homes of two of the staff. Other items, such as dolls, were at Gainsborough Studios at Shepherds Bush, and an exhibition on 'Home Safety' was at the London School of Hygiene. Finally, however, an inventory was agreed and the exhibitions handed over to the National Baby Welfare Council, which had taken over from the NCMCW on 11th July, 1950. From here they were dispersed among various interested bodies, though a permanent exhibition was retained at Gloucester Place. Honora had now relinquished all responsibility for accounts, exhibitions, posters and patterns. The latter were to be named after Margaret Horn, who had visited the office daily to cut them with her own hands until the illness which ended in her death on 9th May, 1949.

Honora had some of the patterns sent to Plas yn Rhiw, where she dealt with orders from Edinburgh, Manchester, Devon and Guy's Hospital. A mention on BBC's Women's Hour brought in more orders, but when they passed on the order from Edinburgh, the NAMCW informed her that they would not stock her patterns in future, as they had their own. Their successors, the NBWC, had no use for them, either. They assumed responsibility for the patterns after Baby Week – 25th June to 1st July. A letter of criticism from North Gloucestershire Technical College, claiming that the patterns were unworkable provided them with a good reason for jettisoning what had probably become impossibly old-fashioned. A few packets of paper patterns remain in the archives.

Among her many preoccupations, Honora retained a strong attachment to Panshanger and its girls. She received news at Christmas, probably in 1947, that Lady Desborough was well and that some of her family were there. The writer recalled Honora's annual Christmas parties. Another correspondent about the same time, thought that Lady Desborough was offering the house to the Ministry of Labour. This must have been refused, as yet another correspondent referred to a recent visit of Honora's in 1951. The following year Lady Desborough died on the 28th of May. A piece in the *Daily Telegraph* for 30th December, 1951, described a fire at the house. Finally *The Manchester Guardian* of 6th February, 1954, described the sale. Honora must have been indeed thankful that she and her sisters had secured Plas yn Rhiw from a similar fate.

The Panshanger 'girls' continued to look to Honora for help and advice. She gave or lent small sums of money, wrote testimonials, supported them in paternity cases and found them jobs. In return they wrote to her with their news and forwarded photographs of her 'grandchildren'. They consulted her in their difficulties over subsequent marriages – should they 'tell'? – should they let their new husbands adopt children of marriages cut short by death in action? Honora wrote back, sympathising, giving good advice, and even holding back from giving advice when it seemed better for a girl to decide for herself. When a girl became involved with the law through her own fault she pointed this out, but didn't withdraw her support. Her correspondence with most girls grew sporadic over time and then ceased, but she continued to write to a few for decades.

Chapter IX

Campaigning

In recommending Colin Gresham to the Keatings as an architect, the National Trust Chairman, F.W. Armitage, introduced them to an enthusiastic member of the Council for the Protection of Rural Wales. They had been in touch with this campaigning organisation at least since 1944, since its aims coincided with theirs for their own part of Wales, but now their commitment became much stronger and deeper. Colin Gresham urged Honora to put herself forward as a member of the committee of the Caernarfonshire Branch which had been formed in the mid '40s. She failed to obtain sufficient votes, but such was Mr Gresham's faith in her that he urged her co-option and in 1948 it was successful. Mrs Cecily Roger Williams-Ellis, the Branch Chairman was uncertain at first whether this would work, fearing that Honora's well-known energy and drive would prove too much for the other members. In the outcome they collaborated well, and Honora served as the Branch Treasurer from February 1951 – February 1953. During this time she designed covers for the Committee's collecting tins, a task which brought her into contact with the artist John Petts, then running the Caseg

Press at Llanystumdwy. Unfortunately he first printed the design, which shows islands off the coast of Llŷn, in reverse. Who was responsible for this mistake is not clear.

The Keating sisters gave their whole-hearted support, which included much practical help and personal inconvenience, to several of the council's campaigns, among the first being a protest against a proposed wind-generator on Mynydd Anelog, at the very tip of the Peninsula. Then as now, feelings were mixed about the project, but the Keatings were unequivocally opposed to the venture on that spot, and in 1952, when some of their neighbours called on them to organise opposition, they were only too happy to oblige. They drew up a petition, they urged visitors to do all they could, and they enlisted the help not only of the CPRW, but of bodies such as the North Wales Hydro-Electric Power Commission and the Commons Open Spaces and Footpaths Preservation Society. (They had already been in touch with the latter over opening up a coastal footpath for Llŷn.) The British Electricity Authority were proposing to set up a compulsory purchase order for the land they needed, and it was hoped to show that this was Common Land.

Individuals were roped in as well. Among them there was their friend, Jeanie Salter, who went to a meeting of Conservative Ladies in Rhyl, which was addressed by Lady Maxwell Fyfe, wife of the Home Secretary and Minister for Welsh Affairs. Mrs Salter managed to speak with her, but was asked to send particulars for Sir David to the Chief Conservative Agent for Wales, an expert piece of buck-passing. She also saw Huw T. Edwards, Chairman of the Welsh Tourist Board and a copy of the information was sent to him. Another staunch ally was William

George, nephew of Earl David Lloyd George and a practising solicitor in Porthmadog. Early in 1952 Honora sent him a report of Mrs Salter's activities and how she had written to Aberdaron parish council. Teresa Hooley also wrote in support of their protest.

In August, *The Western Mail* printed a letter from Moses Griffith, a leading figure in the farming life of Caernarfonshire, showing that the BEA were going back on their promises of local electricity from hydro-electric schemes, which had been hotly opposed by the NWH-EPC. The parallel was obvious, and the conclusion there for the parish councillors to draw.

Before the hearing, at Caernarfon on 3rd October, 1952, the Keatings submitted their written objections to the Compulsory Purchase Order. They came under four headings:

1. The wind generator would destroy the scenery and interfere with the religious associations of the site of an ancient chapel.

2. It would make a mockery of the Keatings' gifts of land to the National Trust in that area.

3. It would be detrimental to the tourist industry which is important to the economy of Llŷn.

4. They would prefer not to have any electricity at this price.

She also objected to the distance of the Caernarfon inquiry from the site – a matter of eighty miles for the round trip for herself and other witnesses. Honora orchestrated the strategy in a draft report to the Caernarfonshire Branch of the CPRW and the NWH-EPC. It was to spring opposition on the Inquiry suddenly and to have different aspects taken up by different groups.

She doesn't seem to have anticipated the outcome, marked as it was by an element of farce. The Inspector had failed to provide an interpreter for the monoglot Welsh witness. The Inquiry was adjourned to Aberdaron on the 14th of November, when an interpreter would be present.

Lord Merthyr, Minister of Fuel and Power, was extremely angry. In correspondence with the Keatings he alleged that the Nationalists had taken over the inquiry and that the 'monoglot witness' had been over-heard conversing in fluent English outside the Inquiry hall. Honora indignantly denied these insinuations and the Keatings redoubled their efforts before the adjourned Inquiry.

The help of the English press was invoked. Mrs Williams-Ellis had a letter published in *Country Life*. Mrs Salter's tackling of Lady Maxwell Fyfe resulted on the one hand in Sir David contacting the Minister of Fuel and Power, and on the other, Honora herself writing to the Chief Conservative Agent for Wales. This drew a protest from the North Wales Group Executive of the Wales and Monmouthshire Conservative Party, with Brigadier Scaife of Dolserau Hall raising the matter at the meeting. Now she wrote to the Northern Correspondent of *The Times*, which published a photo and article on the proposed wind farm on the day of the second inquiry. She admitted that she found the Welsh correspondent of the *Liverpool Daily Post* more knowledgeable. They had to rely on others for reports in the Welsh press.

Other possible allies were Lady Megan Lloyd George, then an MP, and Huw T. Edwards, whom Jeanie Salter felt was on their side when she met him. Hopefully Honora wrote to the Clerk of the Llŷn Rural District Council, drawing his attention to the admission of the BEA Inquiry that there would be no extra electricity for Aberdaron. Despite not taking up his suggestion that 'temporary occupation' of the land was all that was necessary, Honora sought the help of W.H. Williams of the Commons, Footpaths and Open Spaces Society to the extent of offering him hospitality at Aberdaron. The National Trust worked behind the scenes, but the Secretary was not willing to attend nor to allow his assistant to do so. But the local representative was present.

After all this preparation, the great day arrived, with the Inspector, and, this time an interpreter. The evidence was submitted, the witnesses on both sides heard and the Inquiry closed. No conclusion was announced.

The protesters continued their efforts. Honora wrote to the Secretary of the National Trust, giving her account of the proceedings and asking for further help. Mrs Williams-Ellis wrote to the Editor of *The Times*, suggesting that more suitable sites in Scotland could be found. The Ministry of Fuel and Power wrote apologising over the language 'slur' and allowing that the Keatings had a 'real and legitimate interest' in the BEA's proposals. Honora wrote to the BEA, telling them that there were more objectors than they knew about. On the opposing side, *Picture Post*, at that time highly influential, published on 20th December an article in favour of a generator.

On the 17th of December, Honora drafted a letter to the Minister of Fuel and Power expressing her pleasure that the BEA were not going ahead with wind power on Mynydd Anelog. The following day a letter was sent from 10 Downing Street acknowledging an earlier letter and enclosing a copy of the letter to the Minister of Fuel and

Power. To this day no wind generator turns on Mynydd Anelog.

The strenuous campaigning over Anelog brought the Keatings, and Honora especially, into the public arena in Llŷn. At the same time she laboured diligently in private at her work as Treasurer of the Caernarfonshire Branch of the CPRW. She made endless lists of members, chased up those who were late with their subscriptions and prepared annual accounts for the auditors. Something must have gone wrong with these at the beginning of 1953, for in May, Mrs Williams-Ellis was begging her not to resign and arranging for a meeting in Pwllheli. Honora explained that she could not come to Pwllheli then, as it was Fair Week, but invited Mrs Williams-Ellis and Mrs Drage of Cricieth, to come to the Plas. Mrs Williams-Ellis accepted and felt that the matter could be cleared up. Nevertheless, despite another letter begging her not to do so, Honora sent in a letter of resignation in June. She finally resigned in December although the architect, S. Colwyn Foulkes, a member of the committee, wrote to sympathise with her over this 'unpleasantness' with the bank manager. Colin Gresham wrote as Secretary to thank her officially for her work on behalf of the Caernarfonshire Branch.

Despite no longer being Treasurer, Honora continued as a member of the Committee and lent a hand in its minor campaigns. One of these was against the caravans which were spawning over the countryside, destroying the very beauty which their owners were coming there to seek. Honora reported to the Committee on caravan sites at Treheli, immediately below the Plas, Porth Ysgo, on the other side of Mynydd Rhiw, and Bryn Du at Aberdaron. Further afield, she invoked the interest of the Secretary of

CPRW, Mr Herbert Griffin, in the caravans near Porthmadog. In 1957, she represented the CPRW at the inquiry into a caravan site at Crowrach, Llŷn. It was rumoured in the village of Rhiw that the Keatings spent most of their time with binoculars, searching out illegal caravans within range. By 1959 they were even concerning themselves with an inquiry about a caravan site at Mochras, in Ynys Môn. This time the appeal was dismissed. At a similar inquiry in 1958, an appeal for a café and snack bar in Llanbedrog was turned down after strenuous efforts on the Keatings' part.

A large number of letters attest their concern over the removal of sand and shingle from the beaches at Nefyn and Morfa Nefyn from 1957 to 1959. Here again, the CPRW played its part and the extraction was stopped. Even closer to home, the Keatings invoked the help of the CPRW in the removal of a ruined brick building belonging to one of the Armed Services.

Despite her deep commitment, Honora didn't always allow her relationship with the CPRW to run smoothly. In 1953, she disclaimed knowledge of arrangements for the formation of a Porthmadog Group. There is no record of what she made of a new Cricieth group in 1957, when its new secretary introduced himself to her as a vegan who lived mostly on raw vegetables, and sent her a copy of *The Vegan*. In 1953 she ventured to point out errors to Colin Gresham in his Report to the Caernarfonshire Branch.

Nevertheless, the Keatings were stalwart workers for the CPRW, whose efforts were well appreciated. One member of the new Cardiganshire Branch wrote in 1959 that she was glad to have it and knew that the Keatings had worked to help to get it. They also worked for a merger with the Friends of Ardudwy, creating a stronger branch in Meirionnydd.

In the Report of the Caernarfonshire Branch for 1957-8, Honora reported the announcement in August 1957, of an Atomic Power Station to be built near Edern on the north coast of Llŷn. She suggested a petition aiming at 12,000 signatures and leaflet. This campaign was to occupy her and her sisters for the next three years – a more serious threat to the landscape she loved than anything she had known before.

During this period, there were various attempts by the police and by the ITA, to place a mast on top of Mynydd Rhiw. This, again, was a threat to the naturalness and wildness of their world, and the Keating sisters fought it off with all the weapons at their disposal, including the CPRW. At one point, Honora even suggested that the best alternative would be Ynys Enlli, but this was before the formation of the Bardsey Trust and the full recognition of the island as a place of sanctity and natural interest and beauty.

Having finally handed over the deeds of the Plas to the National Trust, the Keating sisters entered on a joint effort to maintain and repair the house and its immediate surroundings, while donating more and more land to preserve in perpetuity for others their enjoyment of the scenic beauty of Llŷn. Especially they hoped in this way to further their aim of fighting off the spawning horror of caravan sites, which had already swallowed up part of the coastline.

When they had bought the house, they had found a torrent entering at the back door, running through the downstairs rooms and leaving by the front. One of their first tasks, therefore, had been to divert the course of this indoor stream. Drainage remained a problem, especially when a new culvert on adjoining property threatened a new deluge. In 1953, one of the first tasks of the new North Wales National Trust agent, H.J. Tetley, was to help them sort this out. Another early precaution against damp was re-pointing, for which they sought the advice of architect, M.T. Pritchard, of Blaenau Ffestiniog on the rough casting. The verandah, too, needed repair and the front of the house was repainted, entailing the frustration of endless delays.

Indoors was enhanced by the purchase of antique furniture from country houses. A typical sale was at Gelliwig – the house which had been the home of Miss Lloyd Edwards, later to become Mrs Gough of Nanhoron – which was sold on Mrs Gough's death in 1953. Here they bought goods to the value of £6.5.0, and Miss Black, Mrs Gough's secretary, wrote from her new home in Essex, that she was glad that they were able to go to the sale, which would have been within walking distance. Other domestic items included the repair and cleaning of a Kelim by a London firm and an auctioneer's offer of a second-hand stair carpet. By 1955, an Esse cooker had been installed in the kitchen and was beginning to give trouble. As usual, Honora went straight to the top – to the makers – and was told that the Liverpool office should arrange for a representative to call.

In 1954, life at the Plas was made much more comfortable by the arrival of electricity and telephone. The route for the electricity supply had been raised by Mr Tetley as early as April 1953, but although Honora had agreed, there had to be negotiations with the Nanhoron estate, resulting in some delay. It must have been a boon not to have to bother with lamps and candles, or have coal carried up to the first floor sitting room. The phone seems not to have made much difference at first to the avalanche of paper going in and out of the house, but its presence would have been a guardian against emergencies, especially since at no time did any of the sisters drive a car.

The woodlands surrounding the Plas occupied much of their thoughts. They sought the best advice available in 1954 – from the Forestry Commission and the Forestry Department at Bangor University College. The following year they grieved over trees that winter gales had brought down and May Sykes wrote to sympathise. In 1955, new anxiety was reflected in a tactful letter of Mr Tetley's, telling them he did not think they should bother Professor Mobbs and that he would look at the trees himself. One tree that particularly bothered them was close to Bryn Ffoulk at the bottom of the hill, standing on Air Ministry land. Though not strictly their concern, they were anxious that it should not be felled. Eventually it had to be taken down, as it was a danger to the cottage. The bad feeling engendered by this episode was increased when the cottage was actually damaged when the Plas trees overhanging the road were lopped.

Part of the agreement with the National Trust was that part of the house and the gardens should be open to visitors for some of the year. This and its inclusion in the 'List of Properties' brought it to the attention of the public, who came in increasing numbers. Every effort was made to enlist visitors as new members: ten were enrolled in 1955. Later the Plas would win awards for the numbers added. Sir Compton McKenzie and James Lees Milne included Rhiw in their books for the National Trust, although Clough Williams-Ellis provoked a protest by omitting it from his first edition. Humbler publicists included the landlady of a Cricieth guest house who always recommended it to her guests. The BBC made a programme about it and the *Liverpool Daily Post* sent a reporter who wrote an article, describing how the Keatings had had the wooden pillars put in the hall, and how they had obtained doors from demolition yards and period furniture from Nottingham. *The Lady* published an article about Sarn cottage which was not being used for holiday lets. The Creuddyn Historical Society paid a visit, as did a party of foreign students brought by Professor Jones Pierce of Aberystwyth.

With this growing fame, Honora decided to write the history of the Plas. With her usual thoroughness she consulted experts such as Professor Jones Pierce who gave her information on the site from its earliest, pre-historic inhabitants, through Merfyn Frych and his descendants, to the Lewis family from whose last remaining member they had bought the Plas. In 1957 she was able to offer visitors a well-produced booklet which was as accurate as she could make it. Disappointingly, she had to relinquish the romantic idea that the space under the medieval staircase was a priest-hole. Previous visitors had been assured that this case was all the more likely since Llŷn was one of the last outposts of the 'Old Religion'.

While the Plas itself was being improved, repaired and opened to the public, the surrounding land became the target of the Keatings' interest. One of their aims was to restore the estate, which had been much depleted in the nineteenth century, to its former extent. With this in view, they attempted to buy land which the Air Ministry had requisitioned before the war for its own bombing school. After protracted negotiations, their solicitors suggested to them in 1958 that the best solution would be a covenant between the owner and the National Trust.

By 1955 they had purchased and donated to the Trust Mynydd y Graig (mynydd: *mountain*; craig: *rock*) a jagged shelf that looks as if the land had sagged perpendicularly down its face, leaving the black teeth grinning. The list of properties for Spring of that year also notes the donation of land at Pen-y-Mynydd on Cilan – another wild place with steep cliffs dropping into the sea, directly opposite the Plas across Porth Neigwl.

With Mynydd y Graig came Syntir, a cottage which was let on a very long lease at a guinea a week. The tenant was (unusually for the Keatings) allowed to sub-let. Eileen advised her to advertise in *The Times* and *Manchester Guardian* for a 'better type of tenant'; presumably following her own practice with regards to Sarn and other cottages which were now let on a short-time basis for holidays. One of these was Bod Sara, and a piece of land near it, purchased in 1953 or 4. In 1954 also, they purchased a piece of land at Llain-y-Morfa, near Llanengan, but this the National Trust refused. On the other hand, they accepted in 1955, land at Maen Ciwm, Tan-yr-Ardd and Parc Twyn Coch, and the formalities for all of these were completed in January 1956. These gifts, 208 acres in all, were to commemorate the 60th Anniversary of the National Trust, but it meant more to the Keatings. The Minister of their church in Nottingham came close to it when he described it as a 'gesture . . . in the grand tradition of our Faith'. It was fulfilment of a duty – to do whatever they could when they saw need. The need here was to preserve the beauty of Llŷn. This they guarded jealously against development, as when a shop was opened on land at Cilan.

Land purchases became a passion with them, and in 1957 they proposed buying more land adjoining the Plas. They succeeded, and the conveyance was executed in March 1958. This land was donated to the National Trust. Unfortunately this gift was not recorded in the List of Properties for July 1958, and their solicitors were instructed to point out this omission for amendment in the next list.

An unexpected ally in this campaign was a retired clergyman, H.T.V. Nunn, who had been used to bringing boys to camps at Abersoch. He was distressed by the state of one of the farms on Cilan and wrote to the Secretary of the National Trust, with a view to its being 'taken over' by that body. He was referred to the Keatings and Honora replied with an account of her own connection with Llŷn, referring him in turn to Mr Tetley and to the CPRW. He was willing to bequeath his own money to keep the spot free of caravans. Eileen seems to have contacted the County Planning Officer, who promised to send his assistant down. Between them, they prevented a caravan park on the site.

The amazing energy of the Keating sisters allowed them to conduct several minor campaigns contemporaneously with their more important ones. The nearest to home concerned the radio mast which the North Wales police wished to erect on the mountain above them – Mynydd Rhiw. They fought it from 1955 to 1959, marshalling their old allies – the CPRW, the National Trust and the Commons, Open Spaces and Footpaths Society, since the site was common land. They protested to the Clerk of Gwynedd Police, the Caernarfonshire County Council and the Ministry of Supply – to no avail. In November 1959, the Gwynedd Police Authority informed them that there was no alternative site.

In Autumn of the same year they were more successful in opposing an ITA mast on the mountain. Again the CPRW and National Trust were involved. By the 23rd of October the *Liverpool Daily Post* announced that ITV were going to explore an alternative site on Mynydd Cenin.

About three miles from the Plas, as the crow flies, stands one of the oldest Nonconformist chapels in Wales – simple and austere, with the pulpit in the middle of one of the longer walls and the pews grouped around it. Nowadays it is surrounded by fields, although when new it was at the centre of a farming community. The story of its founding is a romantic one. The Lady of Nanhoron, Catherine Edwards went, as was her custom, to meet her sailor husband on his return from a tour of duty. She took only enough money for the outward journey, for he would have his pay and bounty money for the journey home. This time she was greeted by sad news. Her husband had died and been buried at sea. She was stranded in Southampton, without money and without male protection. A Nonconformist minister helped her and when she returned, she sold some of her silver to pay for a chapel for those of her tenants and servants who wished to worship in the new way. In 1952, the Secretary of the South Caernarfonshire Congregational Association, the Reverend John Pugh, wrote to the Keatings to ask if they could help the CPRW take it over. The local

Congregationalists were no longer able to meet the expenses of its upkeep. The sisters met this appeal with a sum of money which enabled the building to be restored by T. Alwyn Lloyd and opened to the public. In 1958 they donated a Book of Devotions which is on display.

One of the earliest photographs in the archive is of a dog – standing by himself – to be admired by the family. They always loved animals, and even when they went round shabbily dressed themselves, they found money enough to pay for dog food and vet's bills. Rabbits were not the only animals that had to be killed humanely, when it was necessary to kill. They corresponded with their MP, Goronwy Roberts on the subject of the Jewish slaughter of animals and also on the handling of very young calves. They didn't man barricades, but they wrote to bodies such as the British Union for the Abolition of Vivisection and Animal Reserve Centre at Ringmer and also the local press – *The Caernarvon and Denbigh Herald*. They drew up petitions about the export of live animals, collection of bird eggs and the slaughter of Exmoor ponies, and recruited friends such as Teresa Hooley to collect signatures. By 1957 Eileen was acting as the local Honourable Secretary for the RSPCA. Occasionally their zeal outran their knowledge. A letter to Eileen from *The Guardian* naturalist, William Condry, explained that the 'trapping' and ringing of birds was not harmful to them.

In 1955, the Keatings contributed to the Arts and Crafts Exhibition at the National Eisteddfod in Pwllheli. The following year they entered into correspondence for a hearing at Aberdaron concerning footpaths. Even the emptying of litter bins at Rhiw became the subject of a short campaign in 1957, as did the lack of good music on the Welsh Home Service – the Third Programme was unobtainable.

The indefatigable sisters also conducted campaigns on behalf of individuals, such as the singer Leila Megàne, who was living near Pwllheli. They welcomed her to the Plas and distributed leaflets inviting contributions to her Scholarship Trust Fund. They wrote letters on behalf of a young acquaintance who had failed his exams, to whom they offered help with private tuition fees.

All this was to stand them in good stead when it came to the Big Campaign – Edern.

Chapter X

The Big Campaign – Edern

Honora's experience as Exhibitions organiser for the National Council for Mother and Child Welfare, and as Matron of Panshanger had taught her diplomacy in dealing with officialdom. Her involvement with the CPRW had given her insight into planning campaigns for preserving the beauties of the countryside. The local campaigns against a café and a wind generator on Llŷn had given her a taste for victory. All these were needed in her and her sisters' campaign against the proposal for an atomic power station at Cwmistir, a rocky cove near Edern, on the north coast of the Peninsula.

The late fifties and early sixties saw the most intense activity in the erecting of Britain's nuclear generators. The White Paper of February 1955 outlined a ten-year programme. Although the credit squeeze of 1957 brought deferment of the completion date to 1966, actual building went ahead at Calder Hall in Cumbria and Chapel in Dumfriesshire. Sites remote from concentrations of population were chosen, because their safety was not entirely assured, given the newness of the technology. A further selected site was at Trawsfynydd, in the heart of a wind-swept moor, surrounded by the tiny villages and well spaced-out farmhouses of Meirionnydd.

Few objections were raised. It had housed an army training camp since World War I; it was not a holiday area; and the local population had benefited from the employment afforded by the hydro-electric scheme at Blaenau Ffestiniog. Nevertheless, sufficient opposition was generated to necessitate a public inquiry.

Signs of this opposition were looming in a report to *The Caernarvon and Denbigh Herald* of the 22nd of March 1957, which summarised a parliamentary reply to Cledwyn Hughes, MP for Ynys Môn. David Renton, Parliamentary Secretary to the Ministry of Power announced that there had been nine Welsh requests for Atomic Power Stations. Comparing Atomic Power Stations with earlier hydro-electric schemes, he spoke of the opposition mounted by amenity societies. He ended with a thinly veiled threat: 'It will need the co-operation of all concerned'. Reading this, the Keating sisters may well have felt encouraged to do battle, since the most likely Welsh site to be chosen after Trawsfynydd was Cwmistir, barely seven miles as the crow flies, from their beloved Plas.

The first line of attack was letter-writing. On the 7th September, Honora sent the Minister for Welsh Affairs a leaflet and a letter. It was the precursor of many, including several to the Prime Minister, Harold Macmillan. Honora was used to going to the top. Letters also went to the press, both local and national, countering letters in support of the power station. At the request of Cecily Williams-Ellis, Secretary of the Caernarfonshire branch of the CPRW, Honora wrote to the BBC, asking them to correct a report on Llŷn.

The second attack, following from the first and backing it up, was a petition to be presented to the various ministries concerned. It stated:

We, the undersigned, wish to add our protest against the proposed Atomic Power Station, Edern, as the area is designated as of 'Outstanding Natural Beauty' and is one of the most fertile agricultural districts of North Wales. The native industries of Agriculture and Tourism would be adversely affected by an unsightly erection which would have only a limited period of use as it would become radio-active and unapproachable for demolition.

The first sentence referred to the designation of Llŷn in 1955 as an Area of Outstanding Natural Beauty. In putting this first, the sisters were underlining the difference between the rich, arable land of the peninsula and the windy uplands of Trawsfynydd. The second sentence contains a prediction which has proved only too true. At the time of writing, controversy still rages over the best way to dispose of the decommissioned buildings of Trawsfynydd.

However, in 1957, not many people were giving thought to this difficulty. Unemployment and rural depopulation were more pressing problems. Many of the Keatings' helpers encountered strong opposition. A Rector's wife was told it was all right for her to support the petition: her husband's job was secure. Nevertheless, tea dispensed in the upstairs sitting-room, accompanied by St Ivel cheese and jam Swiss roll, helped to strengthen their resolve.

Copies of the petition were left in village shops and distributed to landladies for their visitors to sign. Some did well and requested more forms. Visitors to the Plas were asked for their signatures. Family and friends wrote in pledging their support.

The sisters found a very useful friend in the owner of the land at Cwmistir, Muriel Penny. She wrote to both Henry Brooke, Minister for Welsh Affairs, and to the National Parks Commission arguing that the project be rejected. She cited its effect on tourism and agriculture, and suggested that another site be chosen, outside an Area of Natural Beauty. She also stressed its vulnerability in war-time, the rights of the individual and the fact that the employment would not be permanent. Later she joined the National Farmers' Union and the Country Landowners' Association, in the hope of influencing these bodies.

By the end of November, the petition was ready, at least in part. Honora wrote to Sir Herbert Griffin, of the CPRW, asking for his help when it was sent up. By the middle of December, it was on its way to the Minister for Welsh Affairs, accompanied by 692 signatures and a covering letter, which reiterated the arguments concerning tourism and agriculture, but also addressed the points made by its opponents concerning unemployment and the loss of the Welsh way of life through depletion of the native population. It emphasised the natural beauty of the area and put forward small industries as a solution for rural unemployment.

Copies of the covering letter were sent to Sir Herbert Griffin, to the National Parks Commission, to the Minister of Power and to the Prime Minister. The Minister of

Power's reply was a masterly piece of stone-walling: no application concerning the site had been received. The reply from the National Parks Commission was the same, but explained that since no application had been received, there could be no Public Inquiry. Nevertheless, the Commission was 'concerned'. Well might it be, for Trawsfynydd was within the Snowdonia National Park, and the inquiry into its future was due to take place at the beginning of 1958.

Here, Honora looked for support from the CPRW, which she had served over the years with ardent loyalty and meticulous attention to detail, but it was lukewarm. It decided not to oppose the Trawsfynydd site. Honora wrote that she was 'heartbroken' over this, but could only hope that it would help over Edern.

As a result of the Inquiry, held from the 12th to the 14th of February, Trawsfynydd was confirmed as the first site in Wales for a nuclear power station, with work due to begin in 1959. It was to become operational four years later.

Meanwhile, the sisters acquired new support. They received a letter from Arthur Blenkinsop MP, later to become Vice President of the Ramblers' Association. He was in favour of creating new employment, but thought it should be on sites of previous industrial development. N.H. Calvert, of the National Parks Commission, was concerned over the Snowdonia National Park and the Llŷn Area of Outstanding Natural Beauty having been chosen as sites for nuclear power stations.

But by far the staunchest ally to join the cause appeared just after the Inquiry. Honora never referred to having attended, and the travelling would have been difficult, unless she managed to obtain a lift. However, she would have known of the North West Hydro-Electric Power Commission through the CPRW. From their opposition to the Atomic Power Station in the Report, she would have realised that here was a body of people, albeit English and outsiders, who felt strongly about the Welsh countryside. She was soon conducting a vigorous correspondence with its chairman, the Rev. H. H. Symonds, and secretary, Colonel Gerald Haythornthwaite.

Initially, the Colonel urged that it should be the CPRW who should lead the fight over Edern. He sent a resolution, worded by the Rev. Symonds, to the Chairman of their Caernarfonshire branch, opposing Edern. At the same time, he hoped the Keatings would continue fighting from their corner, and brought up reinforcements in the form of a letter to the *Liverpool Daily Post*. He invited one of the Keatings to attend a special meeting of the North Wales Sub-Committee, convened at the Queen's Hotel, Chester. The minutes listed a report on the Trawsfynydd Inquiry and a resolution urging that opposition to the Atomic Power site at Edern should be organised as quickly as possible.

Honora was cautious. She pleaded with the Chairman not to publicise English opposition, for fear of a counter-attack from the Welsh. In the same mood, she advised Colonel Haythornthwaite not to involve at this point Colonel Wynne Finch, Lord Lieutenant of the County, whose land ran close to Cwmistir. Although he was in favour of the petition, she preferred to reserve him as one of her big guns.

One of the NWH-EPC's strategies was the production of a leaflet. This involved endless negotiations over a photograph, the caption under it, the date of publication and, above all, the signatories. Honora insisted that they should be local people whose involvement could not be questioned. Another bone of contention was a poem, 'Cwmistir' by a local poet. It was sent to them by their friend, R.S. Thomas, together with an anonymous translation. Honora wanted it included, because she knew that a poem would say more than a picture to a Welshman. In the end, she had to concede that the translation was not of a sufficiently high standard.

The leaflet brought another unexpected ally. A letter in the Welsh-language paper *Y Faner*, from Dr Peate, Keeper of the Welsh Folk Museum at St Fagan's provoked a reply. Diplomatic as ever, Honora wrote to congratulate him – and included a plea for support. This came in the form of a request for a petition form, which Dr Peate filled with signatures from colleagues, friends and neighbours, and staff from the Welsh department of the University College of South Wales, Cardiff. Most notable among these was Saunders Lewis, lecturer in Welsh, playwright and one of the three who in 1936 had protested by setting fire to the proposed bombing school at Penrhos, a few miles away. Their new friend had done well for them, but he also agreed to translate the leaflet into Welsh, essential for full local support.

This was not as readily forth-coming as Honora might have had reason to hope. She had written to the Rev. H.H. Symonds complaining that the CPRW had done 'nothing till recently'. When the NWH-EPC started taking an interest, they deliberately involved the local branch of the CPRW. When its Executive Committee met on the 5th May, they included the item in their Agenda. On the 15th

June, 1958, an emergency meeting of the CPRW Executive in Cardiff passed a resolution: they would oppose Edern unless there was no alternative.

This, at least, was better than the lukewarm response of the National Trust's North Wales representative, H.J.D. Tetley. At first, he merely stated that it was the Trust's policy not to campaign unless its own property was involved. Later, he relented and promised to bring Edern before the National Trust's Committee for Wales.

An even greater disappointment came when the Keatings tried to exploit their Nottingham upbringing as Congregationalists. Honora requested support from the Quarterly meeting in Pwllheli, on the grounds that their parents had been pillars of the local church. The response, as reported in the *Caernarvon and Denbigh Herald*, was 'whole-hearted support' – for the Atomic Power Station at Edern.

In spite of this lack of official support at local level, the campaign went on. Honora prepared leaflets and photographs for a table in the NWH-EPC's tent at the Royal Welsh Show. Saunders Lewis's reference to the Edern site at the National Eisteddfod was reported on the BBC and in the *Liverpool Daily Post*. Eighty more signatures were added. Letters of support as well as opposition appeared in the local and national press. Honora joined in whenever she saw an opportunity.

By the beginning of September, the Keatings were ready to send a further copy of the petition, containing one thousand four hundred and fifty-two signatures, to Lord Mills, Minister of Power. The new covering letter stressed the former points: the beauty of the site, the effect on the tourist industry and the need for small workshops, rather than heavy industry in the district.

Copies went to the Minister of State for Welsh Affairs, to Lord Strang, Chairman of the National Parks Commission and to the Prime Minister. As before, the Minister of Power's reply was that no application for the Edern site had been received from the Central Electricity Generating Board.

This second petition may have been prompted by their opponents' progress. In early May, Twiston Davies wrote to Honora to say that the County Council had authorised its Deputy Planning Officer to have talks with the CEGB about designating the site at Edern for an Atomic Power Station. In June, Muriel Penny, who had written to Lord Cirtrine, Chairman of the CEGB, on the strength of her husband's acquaintance with him, received a letter from the Board; they were asking the Caernarfonshire County Council to designate Edern as a 'Development Area', in order to facilitate their plans. Co-operation was being required.

Furthermore, a counter-petition was being organised, as Honora had feared, in a letter to Colonel Haythornthwaite, written in early May. She named Goronwy Owen, MP for Caernarfonshire, as a possible instigator. The contrasting fates of the two petitions were pictured by a *Liverpool Daily Post* reporter, who visited two villages adjacent to the site. At Tudweiliog, he found the Keatings' petition, with 13 signatures. In the neighbouring village of Edern, hidden by a hill from Cwmistir, the counter-petition had been signed by 2000.

On a smaller scale, a friend reported that the quarry-workers of Penygroes were refusing to sign, on the grounds that the new power-station would provide a new source of employment, to replace their traditional work. A member of the Caernarfonshire branch of CPRW left because of Honora's stand. She was convinced that rural depopulation, if the Atomic Power Stations were not sited at Edern, would mean the ending of the rich home life of the Welsh. Even the Bishop of Bangor, the Right Reverend Gwilym Owen Williams, preached a sermon in support of the Atomic Power Station at Edern.

Yet the tide sometimes swung against it. An article culled from the *Liverpool Daily Post* describing the huge quantities of material used in the building of Hinkley Point, carried a footnote by R. Wall, the CEGB's site engineer. 'Three miles away there are people who have not electricity.' This was heavily underlined by one of the sisters. Later it was taken up by *Punch*, on its cover for 13th January, 1960.

At the Annual General Meeting of the CPRW at Welshpool, on the 8th of November, the President, Lady Megan Lloyd George, spoke of the need for balance between industry and amenity. Sir Herbert Griffin, on the other hand, showed hostility towards the CEGB when he revealed that it had not disclosed at the Trawsfynydd Inquiry, that plutonium would be manufactured there – much more dangerous than making electricity.

A few days later, a conference in Pwllheli between the CEGB, the Local Authorities and South Caernarfonshire New Industries Committee expressed fears about contamination of cooling water or an accident and went on to call for guidance on safety from an independent scientist.

All this was encouraging, but the year ended sadly.

Another expected ally failed to come up to Honora's expectations. The Youth Hostels Association London Region News printed an article by her, but refused to take her side in the dispute, because Edern was not in the Snowdonia National Park. Shocked, she wrote in protest, that from Llŷn she could see 'the whole Snowdonia range as majestic as a panorama of the Alps'.

Colonel Haythornthwaite wrote to thank Honora for the CPRW's sponsorship of the Edern leaflet and to announce the death of the Reverend H.H. Symonds.

Nineteen fifty nine began auspiciously enough. According to the Colonel, the 'pamphlets' were doing well. The Ramblers Association showed interest in Honora's YHA article. The Chairman of the CEGB was sent a photostat of the petition and signatures.

Then came the most encouraging news so far. On 26th February, under the headline, 'New Search for 'A'-site', *The Western Mail* reported that the CEGB had announced five sites to be investigated in Ynys Môn – among them Wylfa – one of which might supersede Edern. The latter had not been nominated earlier, because Ynys Môn had been thought too remote. It was 'now clear that new lines will have to be laid from Edern anyway'. Since 'part of the out-put will have to meet increasing demand for power from the Bangor area, new power lines to serve Bangor will have to be laid'. The spokesman refused to comment on whether opposition had caused the Board to look further afield, but mentioned that the National Parks Commission and 'other bodies' had campaigned vigorously. There would be work for between two and three thousand men for five years, and afterwards for about three hundred and fifty highly skilled workers. The Clerk to Holyhead Urban Council was delighted. 'A project that would create work would be most welcome.' He omitted to comment on the temporary nature of that work.

With this announcement, victory was in sight, but not yet within their grasp; the enemy had not given in. 'It is a shame that grumpy old ladies who have come to this part of the country to live should be up in arms attempting to stop local people from getting the work which they want' complained one local councillor. The new MP, Goronwy Roberts, at a special meeting of the Llŷn Rural District Council in Pwllheli, accused the CPRW of 'giving false impressions to officials of the CEGB and Government departments in London' and of disseminating 'poisonous propaganda' – thereby acknowledging the effectiveness of the Keatings' methods. He thought Edern 'a beautiful project' and rubbished the Keatings' argument in favour of tourism by calling it 'not an industry, simply money to buy a new costume for the wife'. Today, Trawsfynydd functions only as part of the tourist industry, with conducted tours for visitors and cruises on the lake. Even the age-old accusation was trotted out: that some people 'harbour foxes'. Possibly! They were animal lovers.

However, in London, the forces opposed to more nuclear power stations were gathering strength. Lord Wilmot, Minister of Supply in the former Labour Government, spoke about the vast sums of compensation for nuclear accidents, which would have to be found by the tax-payer, as he couldn't contemplate wide-scale production of atomic energy by private enterprise.

Outside parliament, antagonism about Dungeness was helping the opposition to Edern.

Even this did not stop the sisters. Nothing if not tenacious, they set about the task of sending up more 'poisonous propaganda' – seven hundred and ten new signatures, making over two thousand in all. This time the covering letter advocated the use of coal as an alternative in power stations. The petition was again sent to the Ministry of Power, with a copy of the covering letter to the Minister for Welsh Affairs and the Prime Minister. At Colonel Haythornthwaite's suggestion she wrote also to Lord Mills and Lord Hailsham (Lord Privy Seal) informing them. The 'Government Departments in London' were being kept aware of the opposition.

In reply, the Secretary of the CEGB wrote that no decision had yet been taken, but five sites in Ynys Môn were being looked at. It was the Board's policy, where possible, to build new power stations on the sites of old ones. It was as good as an admission that Edern had been dropped, but the sisters did not relax. They entered into a brief correspondence with the Secretary, E.J. Turner, querying the safety of the stations then being built and emphasising the beauty of Edern. Mr Turner foresaw a shortage of coal supplies. Neither he nor they could have contemplated the virtual extinction of the British coal-mining industry.

On 17th June, 1960, they sent a last batch of two hundred and nine signatures to the Minister of Power.

Four days later, the *Liverpool Daily Post* announced that a start would be made on Wylfa in Ynys Môn in two years' time. Even this did not fully reassure the sisters. In letters to Sir Herbert Griffin, Lord Strand and H.M. Abrahams, they expressed pleasure about Edern, but said they would fight on, in case . . . In his letter of congratulation, Colonel Haythornthwaite sounded a sour note – he would have preferred one of the other Ynys Môn sites. He was looking forward to gas-cooled reactors for their greater safety, and thought that only coal-fired power stations should be built until they became a practical reality. Oil- and gas-fired power stations did not come under discussion.

On the 10th of November, the Keatings wrote again to the Minister of Power, averring their continued opposition, but sending no more signatures. The petition was at an end. The Minister replied to Eileen that Wylfa had been chosen because it was marginally more suitable, but building was not to commence until 1963. Then came the sting – Edern had not been abandoned.

About the same time, the Deudraeth District Council began to worry over the unemployment looming up at the end of the building work in Trawsfynydd. One member even proposed buying up the ex-army camp and turning it into a factory. In the event, the tourist industry claimed it for a chalet park and dry-ski slope.

In every campaign, there are losers. One of these was the owner of a holiday home only three-quarters of a mile from Wylfa. He wrote to the sisters in January 1961, complaining that he could not keep the cottage, as the view would be spoilt. Characteristically, when Honora wrote back she advised him on how to protest. Equally typically, she offered him a field they owned near Rhiw as a gift, to build a new cottage.

Mindful of the warning that Edern had not been

abandoned by the Minister of Power, Honora broke her promise and sent another copy of the petition to the Minister of Power in the new Government, the Right Honourable Richard Wood, and others. The answer was the same. The Minister had received no application, but it was still a possibility. The CEGB echoed this and added that the adoption of Advanced Gas Reactors would make no difference.

Thus, the position of the Government and the CEGB had not changed since the beginning of the campaign. The threat to Edern had not been entirely lifted, but had it ever seriously existed? No Inquiry was held, so that the contestants never met in public, and there was no telling what had swayed the outcome. It may have been simply as the CEGB claimed, that Wylfa was more convenient, and Llŷn too remote. After all, the railway-builders of a century earlier had eventually preferred Holyhead. So, had it all been 'a tale of sound and fury, signifying nothing'?

The cost to the sisters had been heavy. Both Eileen and Honora had been seriously ill, and by the end of 1961, Honora was having trouble with her eyes. She must have sat, day after day, in the little study looking out on the woodland, drafting letters to strangers, as well as the many friends and relations. How often she must have dreaded the difficult journey by bus to Caernarfon, for endless committee meetings. Legend even has it that she would take the less comfortable Caernarfon and Trefor bus from Pwllheli in order to help a small company.

But doubt about their stance and their actions never assailed the Keatings. They saw the defence of the natural beauty in which their home was set as a duty. Therefore they had to do it. Though it could not publicly concede defeat, the CEGB, for all its power, may well have been influenced by the scale and fierceness of their opposition. Even if this was not so, it helped to enhance the general feeling that Areas of Outstanding Natural Beauty were not to be adopted for industry. Before the word became devalued, they were upholders of the national heritage.

Chapter XI

Sisters, Family and Friends, 1952-1959

The Keatings were fortunate in that there were three of them, so that if one were ill the other two could share the work of nursing and looking after the house and its visitors, and campaigning. They were frequently ill. A friend wrote that they were never well. Eileen suffered from arthritis so badly that she had at times to take to her bed. Lorna had had a hysterectomy before she was thirty and was suffering increasingly from the gall-bladder trouble which had prompted her to have x-rays at the same time as Honora in 1947, together with minor troubles such as an abscess in her ear. Honora, after her first brush with pneumonia in the Battle of Britain, suffered recurrent attacks. None of this seemed to affect their campaigning, but when Honora broke her arm in early 1952, during the campaign against the projected wind-turbines on Anelog, she was forced to stop writing for three months, at a time when they had no phone. Nevertheless, the campaign went forward.

However, it did prevent her visiting Nottingham to see

Auntie Pop – Mrs Cropper – who was in her eighties and becoming frailer. It was Eileen who had to go and stay for six months to look after her, but early in 1953 she was ill again and Eileen had to return. This time she made arrangements for her aunt to enter a nursing home – where she stayed for three months only, despite having discussed with Eileen the possibility of clearing her house. She even started going out again to collect her rations, while advising her nieces to take Sanatogen against frequent flu attacks. But she was weakening and finally entered another nursing home, run by a Miss Peregrine, who was probably a friend of the family. Now Eileen took responsibility for her care and her estate, clearing out her house and receiving instructions about informing her friends after her death.

She did not die – not, at least, until well after her ninetieth birthday, in November 1955. Eileen ordered a special cake with ninety candles and went to Nottingham to take part in the festivities, which were attended by several members of the family. It was Eileen who wrote hoping that she was better and advising that 'rest would do her good'. The following year, another cousin reported that 'Aunt Alice' was well and said that Eileen was not to provide a large cake for her ninety-first birthday. This time, Eileen did not attend the celebrations, but Auntie Pop continued to write long gossipy letters and to take an interest in their activities.

Aunt Emma, too, was aging and needed looking after. Honora made the journey to Nottingham in 1953 and saw both aunts, but was somewhat at a loss as to what she should do about them. She wrote to Eileen and Lorna that her instructions 'should be tabulated' – she needed the facts 'clearly put down', just as she had had them in her working life. However, she was able to deal with her elderly housekeeper and her insurance – knowing the right officials to approach.

Aunt Emma died in February of the following year, and, as usual, it was Eileen who dealt with the business which followed. A sale catalogue of 'The Orchards', Caythorpe, Aunt Emma's home, is among the documents in the archive with certain items marked. Eileen probably intended to bid for these, but had probably bought what she wanted when clearing the house, before her aunt's death, as Aunt Emma wrote in January, thanking her for a cheque. A newspaper cutting, undated, described a set of Hepplewhite chairs which may be the ones in the hall of the Plas.

Two Keating cousins, Edith and Aline lived in Kent, where Honora visited them occasionally when she was working in London. They kept up a fitful correspondence and also communicated through May Sykes, who stayed for a while in 1950, with Aline. By 1954 the Kentish Mrs Keating was having to sell up her house and her solicitor wrote to Rhiw at the end of 1953 to say that his client was bestowing a chest of drawers and a carpet as a gift to 'my cousins in Wales'. There were also a bookcase with drawers, four small pewter jugs and plates (she had lived for a time in Switzerland) and a large picture with flowers which were to be purchased by the Keatings. By January 1954, a friend wrote to say that she had the things 'ready for them', mentioning specifically the bookcase and chest. In July, May mentioned a visit of Eileen's to Deal, presumably to arrange for the transport of the furniture. A local removal firm wrote to her in August and again in

October about the moving of 'goods from Deal'.

Another connection with the older generation of Keatings, Eliza, was described by a Nottingham cousin John Horrocks, as the 'lady who was your nurse'. She had also nursed their mother and another member of the family – Geoffrey Keating. In 1954, Honora told Eileen that she'd received an 'unfriendly letter' from Eliza, but if there was any coldness between them this had been dissipated by 1956, when she asked the Keatings to keep her will for her as she was getting old and her husband was ill.

That she took a keen interest in them is shown by the fact that she sent them a cutting from the *Nottingham Evening Post* describing some of their activities. Characteristically, they invited her to Rhiw for a holiday – possibly after the death of her husband, as she made no mention of him in her letter of thanks. The following year, she described to them her life as a 'between maid' at the turn of the century.

The frequent visits of Honora and Eileen to Nottingham to see their aged aunts meant that they were able to supervise their properties and keep in touch with their tenants. Eileen was still the chief business manager, and it was to her that the rents came, together with complaints about woodworm in the furniture, a dangerous chimney, rights of light and lavatories in poor condition. By 1956 this had become too burdensome, her arthritis was worse and she asked her old accountant to look after financial matters for her again.

She continued to keep in touch with tenants, and with lettings. In 1957 one advert alone in the Nottingham Evening Post attracted a hundred and six replies, but she didn't open all of them. A tenant who was trying to run a branch of the Berlitz Language School complained to her about the difficulty in obtaining a work permit for a foreigner. A year later, in January 1957, it had to close. In August that year when property in Arkwright Street was transferred to the British Transport Commission, Eileen wrote requesting that one of the tenants should continue and pay a low rent because he was an ex-serviceman.

In 1955, the Keatings requested life membership of the Thoroton Society, named after a local seventeenth century antiquary, who published his 'Antiquities of Nottingham', whose members met for lectures on historical subjects. In 1957, they became 'friends' in perpetuity of High Pavement Chapel. They continued to receive the literature of both societies and so kept up with intellectual and social life of the city – though often, towards the end of their lives, the little blue magazines from High Pavement were left in their wrappers.

Despite the old ties, it was events nearer home that continued to dominate the Keatings' lives. One of these was Lorna's gall-bladder operation. Although she had been cleared of gall-bladder trouble in 1947, removal eventually became necessary and Eileen accompanied her to Liverpool. On the eve of the operation, Honora wrote to her sisters, sending Lorna 'loving thoughts . . . for her ordeal' while Lorna wrote to Eileen expressing her anxieties for Eileen herself. The outcome was a success, for Honora was able to write a month later that she had seen the doctor, who was 'genuinely pleased' that Lorna was feeling better. At the same time Honora recommended to Eileen the Bluecoat shop, the Philharmonic and a bookshop for the times when she was off duty. Lorna made a triumphant return home, but there were many loving, anxious enquiries about her health from friends and relatives for some time.

Honora's health, also, continued to give cause for concern. Apart from the recurring pneumonia, she suffered from a series of nervous breakdowns. In June 1958, she was a patient at Ruthin Castle, then a nursing home, and shortly after was staying with her friend, Jeanie, with whom she had done her nursing training. Jeanie deplored the fact that she insisted on eating eggs, despite her gall-bladder – she had been brought up to consider them 'healthful' – but her advice was mainly about Honora's nervous system. This she noted was 'terribly frayed' – leading to 'bouts' of temper which her sisters should ignore if possible. Her advice was that they should allow her to exhaust herself in the garden. She was paying the price of those fifteen years of overextending herself and especially of the first two years of the War, when she was over-working, under-fed and suffering the continual strain of the bombing. About this time, too, she learnt that she had a cataract – a cruel blow to one who so much loved to read and write.

Life held its compensations. She continued to paint, littering the little downstairs parlour with pots and brushes. In 1954, a friend wrote to wish her good luck with her painting – possibly for a competition, and the same year she bought a ticket for a lecture on Vermeer in Nottingham. The following year she made a visit to London, staying as usual at the United Nursing Services Club. There may have been a medical reason for the visit, but she knew how to combine pleasure with necessary affairs. It may have been on this occasion that she visited the Royal Academy, which would be having its annual summer show. She came away feeling that the two Welsh artists she had seen there – Kyffin Williams and Charles Tunnicliffe – were 'dreary' and 'commonplace'. With hindsight she might have wished to revise this verdict. She also continued to receive letters and news from Panshanger girls even after Panshanger itself had been demolished.

Younger visitors to the Plas are often shocked by seeing fur coats hanging up in the bedrooms. The Keating sisters had been brought up to consider them an indispensable part of their wardrobes – almost as heirlooms. When Auntie Pop had to enter a nursing home she gave her fur coat to Honora and Honora had her photograph taken wearing it. She would not have connected it with the family's love of animals and their work to prevent cruelty.

May Sykes, Eileen's special friend, had been staying near the Keatings in the village of Rhiw. A fine pianist, she had her own grand piano at the Plas, where she would go to play to the sisters. Newly divorced in 1948, she was homeless, so that when cousin Aline wrote to Lorna in May 1949, to ask if she could find someone to go and live with her temporarily, she thought it would suit them both. May promised to go to her as soon as she could and Aline liked her very much. She couldn't stay long. Her daughter, Joy, had gone back to college and May was in London looking after her grand-daughter, Christine. She asked for her things to be sent to her, from a flat she'd taken in Abersoch, but left a coat for Eileen or Lorna. Her next move was with her daughter to Bearsted on the outskirts of Maidstone, from where she wrote frequently to the Keatings, and stayed at their cottage occasionally. Once she took back a dress to alter for Lorna, and shopped for goods they couldn't buy locally. Even in Maidstone she couldn't obtain the St Ivel cheese with which they plied their tea-time guests. In 1958, she moved again to Leeds, not far from Maidstone, where, she told them, she had an apartment and had bought a hundred-year-old piano. Gradually it became more difficult for her to make the long journey to Wales.

Teresa Hooley, childhood friend of the Keatings, continued to correspond regularly, remembering all their birthdays, and sending such acceptable Christmas gifts as a year's subscription to *John O'London's Weekly* and *Punch*. In 1953, she planned an Irish holiday with Honora, but in the event it was Eileen who accompanied her. She was writing a weekly column 'A Poet's Diary' for *The Bridport Messenger* and sent off-prints to the Keatings. In one of them she described a visit to the Plas and some activities while she was there. Another time she was unable to come because of an asthma attack, duly reported in her Diary. She was continuing to publish volumes of verse, which she sent to her friends and in addition she was alternating with Edith Sitwell to provide a poem for a Sunday newspaper.

Another friend of long standing was Hylda, a devout Catholic living in Dublin. Like Teresa Hooley, she corresponded regularly, and met Eileen in Caernarfon, which was reasonably convenient for the Dublin – Holyhead Ferry. In 1955 and 1956 she spend holidays with them, but in 1957 she wrote that she hoped to go to Lourdes in 1958. Again she met Eileen in Caernarfon.

Carlita still kept in touch from Spain, as did Nicole who wrote that she hoped to go to Brazil to try her luck in TV there, but was later prevented by adverse circumstances.

Margaret, their wartime evacuee, was now the mother of four children, while her sister, Doris, had six. The Keatings continued to take an interest in them, sending them letters and occasional gifts. In return, Margaret wrote to them after they had been connected to electricity, urging them to buy a Hoovermatic and a fridge. She hoped they were using a potato-peeler she'd sent. She didn't realise that they had long devised methods of circumventing the lack of these modern amenities.

Among their more recent friends was Douglas Hague, an architect at the Ancient Monuments Commission. He had first come to their notice when working on the Plas for the inventory of the outstanding buildings of Caernarfonshire. Inevitably they struck up a friendship with him and he would write to them about his work. When he was working on the ancient church at Llanengan he asked if he might stay with them for a holiday.

Undoubtedly the best known of their friends was the poet, R.S. Thomas, who first started to come to stay in one of their cottages in 1955, with his wife, the painter Mildred Eldridge, and their son Gwydion. In 1957 he spent August in Sarn cottage, and this became the family's favourite holiday retreat. While writing 'bread-and-butter' letters about mundane details, he often told the sisters of his activities, regaling them with accounts of the wild birds he found and sometimes reared.

Some of their day visitors at this time were Gwilym T. Jones, who hoped to bring Lord Justice Morris over from Borth-y-gest; Dr Mary Richards of Dolgellau, the well-known naturalist, and Edmund Vale, the writer, who wrote to thank the Keatings for a weekend visit by him and his wife. Claud Price, their artist-tenant also came for a holiday and left a painting with them.

Inevitably, the acquisition of land for the National Trust brought with it many of the cottages on the land. These were eminently suited to be let as holiday cottages, most of them being at some distance from other dwellings and having breath-taking views over the land, sea and coast – as far south as Pembrokeshire on a clear day. More and more of the Keatings' time was taken up by letting these cottages for short-term holidays and occasionally on a long-term basis. The wheel had come full-circle. They were working at what they knew best – the renting of property.

Oddly enough, one of their prospective tenants in 1957, was D.O. Jones – the man with the gun. A gift of apples, the year before, may have reminded him of them. At any rate, he wrote to ask if he could have the cottage at 12/- per week. Perhaps he thought better of it, as there is no record of his stay.

In ensuing years, these lets became more and more their preoccupation.

Chapter XII

Declining Years

By 1959, Eileen was 73, Lorna 69 and Honora 67. They had given, or promised to the National Trust, several cottages and many hundred acres of land in an Area of Outstanding Natural Beauty in an effort to preserve that natural beauty from commercial development. They had opposed their neighbours who had seen in just such development, and especially the building of an Atomic Power Station, the economic salvation of an area which was poor by national standards and lacking in the employment which would keep its young people at home to contribute to its future well-being. They were none of them in good health: they might well have been forgiven if they had decided on a quiet and restful old age. That they did not choose this option is characteristic of their inner strength and sense of duty.

The donations to the National Trust continued. Their technique was to appoint estate agents to watch the local newspaper for details of properties coming onto the market. They would then decide whether they were suitable, and if so, put in a bid. Fortunately for them, most of the land they were interested in was fairly useless for agriculture, as they had found when they tried to raise crops on their own land during the war. Mostly it consisted of poor grazing on the top of Mynydd Rhiw, with the broken-down cottages that went with it to make up the small-holdings, or on the steep slopes lower down; part of it was sandy dunes near Llanengan, on the other side of the bay, which gave access to the beach of Porth Neigwl; part was on Cilan head, affording a poor living to the cottagers, who surrounded their crumbling dwellings with all kinds of rural rubbish which in 1960 the National Trust had to clear with the help of volunteers from the Civic Trust.

Not all the land they bought was of this nature. In 1960, they donated a small farm between the Plas and the sea, called Bryn Ffoulk, in memory of their parents, on the centenary of their mother's birth. They were afraid the tenants would be upset at having the National Trust as their landlord, so they kept the transaction secret from them, and donated the rent. With this farm went another track down to the sea, and a ruined fisherman's cottage at their end of Porth Neigwl.

The following year Foel Tŵr came up for sale, and this they were definitely interested in. The 'Tŵr' or tower, forms the lower part of an old windmill, situated appropriately on top of a bald, rounded hill above the village of Mynytho. From here the whole of Bae Ceredigion can be seen in clear weather, with Eryri towards the north. The most glorious play of sunshine and shadow, seascape and mountains causes many people to stop on the road below to observe the ever-changing scenery. The day after the agreement to purchase, Honora wrote announcing it to the Secretary of the National Trust.

Work had to be done on the building to make it safe, but by October 1963 the Deed of Gift was ready to sign.

A similar pattern developed over the next five years. The advent of Enterprise Neptune in 1966 spurred the sisters to further giving. Penrallt, a larger farm, and Llain y Morfa at Llanengan, and Mynydd Bach were all donated to the Trust outright. Eileen's death, the same year, inspired the donation of land in her memory at Llanfaelrhys and Porth Ysgo, again with a path to the sea, past the old lead and manganese mines.

Matters did not always go smoothly, however. The Trust was reluctant at first to accept Mynydd Bach, because a law-suit was pending concerning a right of way. It took four years to settle, but the result was a happy one, since the handing-over coincided with the year of inauguration of Enterprise Neptune – the Trust's drive to secure as much of the coastline of Britain as possible from the threat of harmful development.

The outcome was not as happy at Tyn y Parc, on the eastward flank of Mynydd Rhiw, which had been purchased by Honora's London GP, Dr Richards. She sold the land to the Forestry Commission, and despite the attempts of the Keatings and the Trust to come to some accommodation with them, they covered vast stretches with highly visible, totally alien conifers. Periodically these failed to thrive in the rough winds of Llŷn winters, but hung on, a gloomy backdrop to a fertile and varied part of the peninsula. Another thorn in the flesh of the Keatings was the caravan park at Treheli, immediately below them, over which they were equally helpless, as planning permission had been given earlier and the farm was not for sale.

All this giving entailed much legal work, not only in the original purchase, conveyancing and handing over, but in matters such as rates, insurance and inventories. Wills had to be altered and Memorandums of Wishes drawn up. Funds had to be provided for the maintenance of the properties, and this occasionally involved the sale of some of their property in Nottingham. Nevertheless, the work was faced and carried out. Sacrifices became evident in the appearance of the sisters. The smart young ladies who had first come on holiday to the area gradually became old women in musty, long overcoats covering clothes that had been fashionable decades before. Some were given them by their friends, altered when possible. Yet these old clothes never detracted from their dignity, nor held them back from their orgy of giving.

Closer to home, the Plas estate itself claimed much of their attention. Their aim was to restore the estate to its full extent in the past, and to this end they purchased the relevant land, including land compulsorily purchased before the War as part of the RAF bombing range. This land, together with house and garden needed much attention.

One of their fears was that a police mast would be erected on Rhiw and there were rumours that fed these fears. Having fought the threat of an Atomic Power Station at Edern, and an ITV mast on Rhiw, they set about mounting another campaign. They would even have preferred a radar station, but this time they were not successful, and the mast now dominates the landscape as one looks across from Mynytho. Equally unsuccessful was their protest against low-flying aircraft, which still periodically pierce the air above the Plas.

Apart from these campaigns, there was the usual upkeep of the house and estate to be overseen. The rabbits were still giving trouble. The National Trust sent a contribution to the Llŷn Pest Destruction Society on their behalf in 1962. The Trust also paid for the external painting of the house in 1960, but the Keatings had to satisfy themselves with the work and make their comments direct to the architect, M.T. Pritchard of Blaenau Ffestiniog. During the sixties the plastering of the 'white house' which had been mentioned by earlier visitors was removed, to transform what had been externally an eighteenth century villa into a stone-built house, reminiscent of an earlier date, more in keeping with the thick end walls which suggested a medieval origin.

In the house, life was made much easier by the advent of electricity and telephone. A bill from Electrolux for a service suggests that their vacuum was well used, as was the phone, with the substantial quarterly bill of £10.12.0. A letter from another friend described to Lorna the effect of their central heating on furniture and the need for proper humidifiers. The system was fed from an enormous boiler in a corner of the kitchen. Grocers' bills for China tea, Players, Marie biscuits, pineapple, Swiss rolls, ginger nuts and fruit drops tell of some of their edible comforts. A request to the Postmaster for books of stamps 'by the postman' shows them well organised for supplies that were almost equally essential to their lifestyle.

It was during the early sixties, too, that the Plas was more publicised. Writing of 'The Quiet Land of Lleyn' in *Country Life* in April 1961, Geoffrey Grigson included a photograph of the exterior of the house. The following year, Edgar J. Jones, the Vicar of Bodedern in Ynys Môn, sent them a copy of his translation of an article on *The Old Chapel*, a building detached from the Plas itself but adjacent to it. In 1964 Bernard Gill wrote about Sarn cottage in *The Lady* under the title 'A Cottage in Wales' and in 1965 there was an edition of two thousand copies of Honora's own book.

Visitors came in growing numbers, including parties such as the Anglesey Antiquarian and Field Club, who were entertained to tea. Other enquiries were not so welcome, such as the offer of embroidered badges by a commercial firm who had seen the address in the 1962 edition of 'Historic Houses, Castles and Gardens'.

The garden at Plas was Honora's particular interest, which continued to the end of her life. In 1961 the work was made easier by the purchase of a Beaver Motor scythe, and later she adopted a philosophy of allowing weeds to grow among the garden plants since they added to the beauty of the garden. She continued to receive catalogues from and place orders with leading nurseries such as Pennells and Hilliers, but her closest tie was with Bodnant. She conducted a continuing correspondence with its famous head gardener, Charles Puddle and bought from him at least until 1972. She turned for advice to the National Trust's Gardens Advisor, who reassured her in 1974 that unsuitable pruning wouldn't do much harm and congratulated her on the well-being of her magnolia mollicomata in such a windy garden. This, as it now is, offered even in winter a colourful refuge from a turbulent world outside, is mainly the result of her labour and creativity.

While Honora exhausted herself in the garden, Eileen

continued correspondence with family and friends in Nottingham and elsewhere. Her chief care was 'Auntie Pop' who was becoming more difficult, and needing more and more care. August 1961, a Sister in Nottingham General Hospital wrote saying that Mrs Cropper was recovering there after an accident. That same year, Eileen ordered a cake for her aunt's 97th birthday but couldn't attend because she'd fallen and broken her arm. A friend blamed a cat.

After this the old lady became more and more difficult. At one point she complained to the Red Cross, and convinced them that she was being badly treated by the Keatings. Several times Miss Peregrine, who ran the nursing home where she was residing, wrote to Eileen with complaints against her aunt. By April 1962, these came to a head, when she stated that she couldn't keep her any longer and had asked the doctor to find another home for her. By May, Eileen had received power of attorney to act for her and from that time, though there were more complaints, there was no talk of her moving. Probably matters were adjusted when Miss Peregrine asked for a rise in payment to ten guineas a week, in view of the trouble Mrs Cropper was giving her. When she died, in October of that year, it fell to Eileen to arrange the funeral and distribute the legacies, ranging from small personal effects, to money left to St Buddock's in Falmouth.

Eileen's visits to Nottingham involved coming into contact with friends of her aunt's, such as Eliza Hooke, whose removal to Battle was deeply felt by 'Auntie Pop', and Olive Ferris, who held power of attorney for her before Eileen. She corresponded also with members of the extensive Keating and Wood clans, such as John Horrocks and his wife Rae, who visited regularly. John Horrocks, an accountant, also took over their finances, continuing to do so after Eileen's death.

Her two lifelong friends, May Sykes and Teresa Hooley still figured importantly in the lives of Eileen and her sisters. May still had no permanent home of her own, but resided sometimes with her daughter, Joy, in London and later in Kent, and sometimes in rented accommodation, occasionally occupying Sarn cottage, though Honora warned Eileen not to spend too much time on her there. She would write long letters describing family matters. Once, when Joy told Eileen how unhappy her daughter Christine was at her school, the sisters offered to pay her fees at another school, but the offer was not accepted.

By 1963, Mrs Sykes had a flat in Beaumaris, in the house of another friend, Jane Bennett. Here she was within visiting distance of her friends and once, at least Eileen went to Beaumaris to see her. Unfortunately, Eileen caught a chill and passed it on to her sisters; but there were further visits and many letters. During this period too, May altered clothes for Eileen and Honora, and made a nightie for Eileen. In return, the sisters had a phone installed in May's flat as a birthday present, but despite Eileen's letter to the engineer in charge of phones at Bangor, she was forced to share the line with her landlady. This was not a happy arrangement, as relations between them grew tense. Miss Bennett expressed resentment against both May and Plas and although she later asked forgiveness, May felt her tenancy was insecure. A few months before Eileen's death she wrote to her expressing her love for the way in which Eileen had enriched her life. Although she continued to write to Lorna and Honora her letters became more formal and fewer.

Teresa Hooley, now back in Derbyshire and resuming her maiden name, was continuing to write and give talks to women's organisations. Besides publishing several volumes of verse, she was contributing a weekly 'Poet's Diary' to a local newspaper, *The Bridport Messenger*. In it she described a visit to Plas in June 1961 when she had read R.S. Thomas's 'Poetry for Supper' and on another occasion she narrated how Eileen had turned up in Nottingham to visit an aged aunt. Naturally she sent off-prints to the Plas.

Her letters were shorter than May's, often no more than a post-card. In one dated 1963, she mentioned her friendship with Clifford Dyment, another Nottinghamshire poet, and at the same time said she was packing up her books and giving them away. She was donating her own works to Derby Borough Library who were making a collection of Derbyshire writers. In another letter, she mentioned that she had taken sweets to the local school children at Christmas. When the Keatings did this at Rhiw, it was not appreciated. The local parents felt they were quite able to provide sweets for their own children. Teresa's Christmas gifts to the Keatings were usually subscriptions to magazines such as *Punch* and *The Countryman* while they in turn sent flowers from their woods. In her last letter to Eileen, a few months before her death, she looked forward to seeing her soon. Despite suffering from asthma, and enduring many difficulties with her husband and son, Teresa survived until 1973.

The Keatings' French 'family' whom they had known almost as long as Teresa, continued to keep in touch, especially with Eileen. Colette decided to retire in 1960, at the age of 84, but the two families continued to exchange gifts and greetings at Christmas and to send news of their respective 'tribes'. Nicole, now married, was still visiting Bréhat with her husband and his eldest son. A few weeks before Eileen's death, Colette wrote to thank her for the booklet on Plas.

Many other old friends kept in touch, but there were newer ones, too. Among these was their evacuee, Margaret, who confided her difficulties with her children and moving house. The Keatings, always ready with financial help, opened a bank account for her, but kept a strict eye on her use of it! In 1960 Honora practised her first letter on the typewriter on her, saying she was looking forward to a visit, but in 1963 she was unable to come. Her parents, Mr and Mrs Hodson and her sister, Doris, regularly sent birthday cards and kept them informed of new additions to the family.

Not so intimate but better known, was Douglas Hague who continued to write and to visit the sisters whenever he was in the vicinity. While excavating the monolithic remains at St Tudwal's in February 1962, he mentioned snow – almost unheard of on the island. Another excavation at Rhiw itself, brought him on a longer visit in 1968, when he stayed at one of the Plas cottages.

As with Margaret, the sisters made friends with his family, especially his wife, Degarry. They were the ones she turned to in 1962, when she felt her marriage falling apart, as her husband spent more and more time with Rosemary Christie, the mother of the actress, Julie. As so often, when friends turned to them in trouble, they invited her to stay and she continued to confide in them, especially when she was worried about her son being invited to live with Douglas. Despite this, they remained friends with him, too.

Although disappointed at not being asked to serve on the committee for Ynys Enlli, Honora took a keen interest in the island, receiving its reports over the years. Through this she met William Condry, contributor to *The Guardian*'s 'Country Diary' column and warden of the RSPB bird sanctuary at Ynys-hir on the Dyfi estuary. In 1954, he brought the new vicar, the Reverend R.S. Thomas and his wife to meet the Keatings. At that time R.S. Thomas had only one book to his credit, the privately published, 'Stones of the Field', but the following year, 'Poetry for Supper' was published by Faber and Faber. From this introduction sprang a friendship that was to last for the lifetimes of all the sisters.

At first, the Thomas's with their son, Gwydion rented different cottages during August, but soon came to prefer Frondeg. By 1960 they were renting it permanently, and the following year they were considering buying it for their retirement. It proved to be too expensive, but the Keatings came up with a different proposal. Sarn-y-Plas, the cottage at the bottom of their hill, was used only for holiday lets; they suggested that the Thomas's should have a lease on it for their lifetime and that their son; after that it would pass to the National Trust. The Thomas's accepted gratefully for they found peace at Rhiw, according to Condry, and both assured the sisters that Rhiw went into their poetry and painting.

For their part, the Keatings followed the growing reputation of their tenant with great interest, collecting reviews of his work from the *Observer* and *Sunday Times* and listening to programmes about him on the wireless.

Teresa read 'Poetry for Supper', published in 1958, with them and another friend travelled all the way to London for a reading of his work. 'Tares', 'Bread of Truth' and 'Pieta' all followed before 1966, but neither of the Thomas's mentioned any of them in their letters. Instead, Ronald usually wrote of bird-watching, and sometimes his parishioners, while Elsi wrote of more practical matters such as Gwydion's career at school and his exhibition to Oxford, cider-making, supplies of milk and bread for their stays at the cottage, or wishing them speedy recovery from their many ailments.

Meantime in Nottingham, the Keatings became involved in a campaign on home ground. Their home, the Old Vicarage in Crammer Street had become a subject of dispute with the Council, who wished to keep it residential. The Keatings wished to turn it into offices, and appealed against the Council's decision. At a hearing in March, the decision went against them and they decided to sell. Friends feared the property might go to coloured people and this may have influenced them in changing their minds. At any rate, they decided to move in one of their tenants, with her six children, and sell her house in St Ann's Hill Road. This was not entirely satisfactory, as the council refused to allow anyone to sleep on the top floor, and the neighbours were not pleased to have five lively boys living in their proximity. Eileen did her best by suggesting that one of the sitting rooms could be turned into a bedroom for three of the boys.

However, it was not long after this that Eileen had the fall which led to her death. Her health had been declining for some time: the rheumatism which had dogged her in the thirties was exacerbated by the damp of the house, especially in the early days, before the central heating. In 1960, Hilda Presley of Nottingham commiserated with her over her leg and late in 1962 she had a bad fall. Characteristically she waited a week before calling the doctor. Teresa scolded her and enjoined 'rallentando', reminding her that she herself was seventy-five, two years younger than her friend. However, Eileen was too preoccupied with the life of the Plas and her duties as business manager for Rhiw and Nottingham to be able to slow down, until she was forced to early in 1965 by a serious operation. Honora could probably see her sister failing, for by the end of 1965 she was impressing on their solicitors the urgency of remaking their wills. At the beginning of 1966, Teresa was looking forward to seeing her again, but the fall brought about her sudden death a few days later.

Unfortunately she didn't live to see the fulfilment of one of her wishes – to have the Thomas's permanently installed in Llŷn. The thought had been with her two years earlier, when the living of Tudweiliog became vacant, but Ronald turned down the suggestion. For him it had the insuperable difficulty of having to live far from his parishioners. Now the living of Aberdaron was about to become vacant, and despite his diffidence about his fluency in Welsh, and urged on by a fellow student at Bangor, the Reverend J.H. Vevar, who was Rector of neighbouring parishes, he went to see the Bishop, and was appointed. Now the remaining sisters had him and his wife as neighbours, even when they weren't at the retreat in Sarn.

Many small kindnesses were exchanged between the two families – the sisters gave flowers to the church and gifts at Christmas, while the Thomas's helped with jobs they couldn't do for themselves. In Lorna's last lonely years, Ronald would make fairy cakes and take them up to her. Possibly the sisters tried their friends in many ways. One story tells how Lorna rang Mrs Thomas, who was busy baking. She answered the phone, then laid it on the table while she went on with her work. At the end of half an hour she picked it up, and Lorna was still talking.

Up to Eileen's death, Honora had continued with many of her former interests. She had even visited the Chelsea Flower Show in 1963, staying at the Women's Farm and Garden Association's premises. Two years later, the WFGA Bulletin incorporated one of her drawings and an article about the Keatings. During this visit to London, she had tea with the widowed Lady Cynthia. She even kept in touch with the Institute of Infant Welfare Fund and also some of her Panshanger girls, who wrote giving details of their new lives and their growing 'babies'.

Nearer home, she entered into many local activities. She subscribed to the Caernarfonshire Voluntary Care Association, participated in the BBC's Audience Research, acted as Auxiliary Secretary for Rhiw of the West Caernarfonshire and Ynys Môn branch of the RSPCA. She received many calls on her time and interest: she was asked to help with a coffee morning at Abersoch for the Royal UK Beneficent Association, and more personally, helped people claim financial assistance from it.

After Eileen's death, these activities became fewer, as both sisters aged and struggled to fulfil the duties she had carried out so meticulously. Although Honora had earlier received a second-hand typewriter as a present, her enthusiasm for it soon waned and she continued to draft her letters in longhand. The typewriter might have helped, but probably the number of 'final demands' from the Inland Revenue would have continued to increase, if one indication of their methods is typical: long after Lorna's death a letter to an accountant was found at the back of her drawer. A high point of these years between Eileen's death and Honora's was the making and broadcasting of a programme on Thames TV in the series 'A Place in the Country' in 1973. Both sisters are shown, eagerly pointing out the beauties of house and garden, and recounting the history of their association with the Plas. Gradually, though, their activities became more confined as various illnesses beset them. With their affairs in Nottingham in the hands of solicitors and accountants, they spent more of their time on managing such of the Rhiw property as they had not conveyed to the National Trust. This consisted mainly of letting the houses as holiday cottages. Honora advertised in *The Times* as she felt this brought 'a better kind of tenant', and also answered advertisements for a neighbour who found it difficult to write in English. Ironically, their lives replicated in Wales their early years in Nottingham, when their mother's chief income had come from property.

This joint period came to an end in 1978, when Honora suffered a fall and died in the Caernarfon and Anglesey Hospital, Bangor, a few days later, at the age of seventy-five. The youngest of the three sisters, she had led a more active life, and the strain of her war-time activities had drained much of her vitality, so that she died at a younger age that either Lorna or Eileen. She was buried at Llanfaelrhys, with her mother and sister.

Left alone, Lorna continued to live at the Plas, coping

extremely well in the circumstances. With little help in the house, except for a woman who came in once a week to clean, it was not surprising that the house was in rather a chaotic state when the National Trust took it over. On the other hand, she managed her finances herself through long telephone conversations with her solicitor on Sunday evenings. Though the sisters had never had a car, or learnt to drive, Lorna bought a car for a friend, who in return chauffeured her when she had need. A life-long talent for making friends allowed her still to welcome visitors to the Plas.

She died in the cottage hospital at Bryn Beryl, outside Pwllheli, in 1981, after a short illness. In her last letter to Mrs J.H. Vevar, she says that she has everything she wants, she is so well looked after. In her will, she remembered the evacuee, Margaret and the friend who had chauffeured her in the last years. This regard for people made her contribution to the work of the trio, if not conspicuous, a vital one.

Lorna, too, is buried overlooking the sea at Llanfaelrhys.

Chapter XIII

The Legacy

In 1948, the Keatings began negotiations to make over their home and its immediate surroundings to the nation, through the National Trust. Though their immediate aim was to preserve in perpetuity an old Welsh manor-house which they had rescued from imminent ruin, by the time the last sister died, in 1981, their achievement and consequent bequest was much greater. They left their mark, physically and spiritually on the whole of the Llŷn Peninsula, which they had come to love with a passion that is usually reserved for one's native hearth. That they had the means to further that love is fortunate for a small corner of Britain that is still relatively unspoilt – in part because of their endeavours.

When one thinks of the Keatings, one thinks first and foremost of the Plas, almost derelict in 1938, declined from its former glory as the home of one of the leading families of the Peninsula. Despite the torrents that flowed through from back door to the front, they restored it to a habitable dwelling. Today thousands of visitors annually enjoy the well-proportioned main hall, the little parlour leading off it, the huge kitchen where servants bustled in former years. Mounting the eighteenth-century staircase they gaze at the first-floor parlour, where visitors were entertained to the traditional tea, St Ivel cheese and Swiss roll. They can peep at the small study next-door, where Honora wrote her myriad letters; they can see the small bedroom with its gloves and hat left on the bed, as if the occupant had just thrown them down after coming home from Church. Up another flight of stairs they are confronted by the medicine cabinet, a grim reminder of illnesses for which there was finally no cure, and a large bedroom, whose furniture is hung with fur coats, a reminder of the smart young ladies who originally holidayed in Aberdaron and Rhiw.

Throughout the house there are ornaments and artefacts that reflect the various facets of the lives of the sisters. In the hall is a painting of Aunt Emma Keating as a girl and Chippendale-style chairs from their old house. In all the rooms there are ceramics, mostly Continental, surviving from the travels of Eileen and Lorna and the Exhibitions mounted by Honora. Her own paintings line the stair and the upper landing, their subjects mainly local, though one portrays an olive grove in Italy. Other objects came from family and friends, while some of the furniture is booty from their forays to country-house sales. The Japanese prints and paintings area reminder of Honora's voyage to the Far East and her particular interest in Japanese art.

Perhaps the most intriguing part of the house to the visitor is the spiral staircase in the thickness of the end wall, which connects the first floor with the second. The bottom flight is missing. The Keatings told their earlier visitors that this was a priest's hole, a supposition made probable by the lingering of the Old Faith in this remote part of the country. Though later research suggests there had been a staircase which was removed when the house was enlarged in the eighteenth-century, the sheer unlikelihood of a stairway commencing in mid-air attracts attention, especially in children.

The interior has a harmonious atmosphere which draws visitors back for repeated visits, but the exterior is more ambiguous. Some time in the sixties, the rendering was removed, causing the house to shed its appearance of a Regency villa. Instead, the granite of the underlying structure is revealed, together with the lines showing where the roof was raised to create a third storey. These sit uneasily with the verandah which runs along the front of the building.

The garden, likewise, is a mixture of styles, the main structure as it stands, being provided by the box hedges which were planted in the early twentieth century, to give protection to the tender plants that grow there. Some of the plants Honora purchased have disappeared, but others remain. Notably the Zephire Drouhin roses clothing the pillars of the verandah give pleasure to the senses of sight and smell. Walking the grass paths between the box hedges, inhaling their foxy smell and viewing the flowers in the little plots between is another sensual joy.

Beyond the house and garden lies the Plas estate, which the Keatings laboured to restore to its fullest extent, before bad debts in the nineteenth-century forced the sale of large parts of the land. The woods above and below, with their drifts of snowdrops, daffodils and bluebells draw many viewers, even early in the year before the house and garden are open.

Below the main road leading to Pwllheli, land purchased from the Air Ministry gives public access to the beach at the western end of Porth Neigwl; at the other end, the sandy warrens of Llanengan provide another path to the sea. Cilan Headland, overlooking the bay, has miles of public pathways through bracken, gorse and heather. Above the Plas, the mountain is open to the public, as is Mynydd y Graig and Penymynydd on the other side of the village. Both afford heart-stopping views of Eryri, Bae Ceredigion, Ynysoedd Gwylanod and Ynys Enlli.

Further afield, the gifts of the Keatings also allow walkers free access. At Anelog and Mynydd Mawr, and at Porth Orion sheep tracks have been trodden into wider paths, including parts of the Coastal path along the northern coast of Gwynedd.

These tangible gifts of the Keatings to Llŷn have encouraged the National Trust to make wider purchases. Most notable is the recent acquisition of the romantic village of Porthdinllaen, snuggling picturesquely into the cliffs near Morfa Nefyn. This, in turn, has inspired the placing underground of cables visible on the land above, an undertaking the Keatings had urged when electricity was first taken across their property. Similarly, the removal of the cicatrice of black conifers form the flank of Mynydd Rhiw, which would never have been there had they obtained their wish of preventing, or at least limiting, the planting in the first place.

What they in all likelihood helped to prevent, was the building of an atomic power station near Edern. Though they were reviled at the time for their stance, even their opponents are now forced to acknowledge their wisdom, especially as they have witnessed the decommissioning of the Magnox station at Trawsfynydd, with its consequent unemployment. This, together with their efforts to prevent the unregulated spread of caravan sites, though often ridiculed, has meant that Llŷn attracts a growing number of visitors, who more and more appreciate its unspoilt beauty.

Since their deaths, the landscape of Llŷn had been more and more appreciated by the inhabitants themselves. The authorities which regulate the numbers of caravans on a site are no longer regarded as busybodies, except by the owners of such sites. Those who seek to safeguard the beauty which is here are backed up by the public, as when the Air Ministry sought to extend the radar station on Rhiw. This too is part of their legacy.

When the APS was under discussion, alternative sources of employment were canvassed. The Keatings advocated market gardening to take advantage of the equable climate, and small craft industries. Unfortunately, these have not been developed as successfully as they had hoped. Individual farmers sell vegetable crops locally, but there is no large-scale growing. The remoteness from large markets has been blamed. Small craftsmen work all over the peninsula, but they rarely employ others.

A more personal legacy is the memory of the Keatings themselves, going back to the early years of the century. Many stories are told of their eccentricities – almost to the extent of a joint paranoia. On the other hand, there are many who speak of their unpublicised kindness. There are no tales of ghosts connected with the Plas, but many visitors speak of a kindly spirit which lingers there.

Some of this kindness was directed to artists and poets such as R.S. Thomas and his wife Mildred Eldridge, to give her her professional name. Without their kindness over the cottage, the world might have lacked some of their work. The friendship and support given throughout sixty years of acquaintance may have been instrumental in inspiring the work of Teresa Hooley, forgotten or derided in the nineties, but highly thought of before World War II. Jonah Jones, whose sculpture enhances many a Welsh scene, was indebted to them for his recovery from an illness which could have proved fatal. As patrons of the arts, they may not have been able to achieve as much as the Davies sisters of Gregynog, but their aim was the same and the result not inconsiderable.

Finally, there are all these lives whom Honora reached through her work. There is no way of measuring how many young mothers were reassured, how many babies were brought up more healthily through her teachings. Neither can one gauge her effect on the young women who passed through her hands at Panshanger, finding practical kindness and understanding when they were most vulnerable.

As individuals, the Keating sisters may have quarrelled and grumbled, but as a team they worked superbly well to serve their generation and the corner of the country where fate had led them. Fortunately there are those qualified and prepared to carry on the work and make the best of their legacy.

Other titles on Llŷn

Llŷn
Elfed Gruffydd
£6.50

**The Llŷn
Peninsula Mines**
Wil Williams
£3.00

Tomos o Enlli
Jennie Jones
£4.00

This Valley was ours
Eileen M. Webb
£7.50

ardal guides

WELCOME TO WALES

Enjoy the rich heritage
and follow the guide
to many attractions of
each *ardal* (location)
of your choice when
you visit Wales.

Price: £3.50 each

WALKS WITH HISTORY

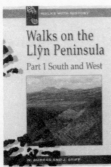

WALKS ON THE LLŶN PENINSULA PART 1 - SOUTH & WEST
N. Burras & J. Stiff
£4.50

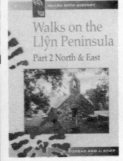

WALKS ON THE LLŶN PENINSULA PART 2 - NORTH & EAST
N. Burras & J. Stiff
£4.50

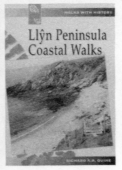

LLŶN PENINSULA COASTAL WALKS
Richard Quinn
£4.50

WALKING LLŶN'S SHORELINE
Dafydd Meirion
£4.95